GET IT
DONE
NOW!

Other books by Brian Tracy

———————

Entrepreneurship

Make More Money

The Science of Influence

The Science of Money

The Science of Motivation

The Phoenix Transformation

The 10 Qualities of Influential People

GET IT DONE NOW!

Own Your Time, Take Back Your Life

BRIAN TRACY

MEDIA

MEDIA

Published 2022 by Gildan Media LLC
aka G&D Media
www.GandDmedia.com

Front cover design by David Rheinhardt of Pyrographx

Interior design by Meghan Day Healey of Story Horse, LLC

Library of Congress Cataloging-in-Publication Data is available upon request

ISBN: 978-1-7225-0580-6

10 9 8 7 6 5 4 3 2 1

Contents

Introduction

⌒

There is a quote attributed to that most famous of individuals—anonymous—that says, "Starve your distraction, and feed your focus." This is the perfect idea with which to open this book.

We live in the most technologically advanced period of history, yet the challenge of remaining optimally productive in our modern world has, in many ways, never been greater. How can this be?

With the advent of mobile phones, killer apps, broadband Internet speeds that stagger the imagination, and nearly any bit of information or product or solution available one click away, how can it be that remaining optimally productive is such a challenge for so many people? How is it that all of these technological tools have not freed us up to focus on the most important items for our professional and personal lives?

The question can be answered with one word: distraction. This amazing technology comes with a dark side. Many of us spend precious time focusing on precisely the wrong things. This goes far beyond trivia, gossip, supposedly urgent news headlines, and the like. I'm talking about the incessant and numerous emails, texts, notifications, and ads that seem important, even urgent, but in reality only complicate our lives and take us further from our goals.

If you are like most people today, you are overwhelmed with too much to do and too little time. As you struggle to catch up, new tasks and responsibilities keep rolling in like the waves of the ocean. Because of this, you will never be able to do everything you have to do. You will never be caught up. You will always be behind in some of your tasks and responsibilities, probably in many of them. For this reason, perhaps more than ever before, your ability to select your most important task at each moment, and then to get started on that task and get it done both quickly and well, will probably have more of an impact on your success than any other quality or skill you can develop.

In this book, I will discuss a variety of mental approaches, skills, and strategies to enable you to select that most important task at each moment and get it done on schedule. You'll learn some of the greatest time-saving methods ever conceived; how to get organized and stay organized; why you should plan every day in advance; the difference between bad procrastination, which you should avoid, and creative procrastination, which I endorse wholeheartedly; productivity tips for the workplace and the home; and more.

Here you'll discover that there truly is a science to productivity—a science that has been tested and proven again and again, not just for years, but for decades, with landmark publications like *The Effective Executive* by Peter Drucker and my own books, *Time Power* and *Eat That Frog*.

Today we have more sophisticated data on time management and productivity than ever before, with details on how people actually spend their time in the workplace versus how they believe they are spending their time. I'll present some of those findings in this book, and they will shock you.

The goal of this book is to bring you many of the verified facts about productivity, eliminate the myths and half-formed theories, and leave you with a treasure of ideas for becoming more influential in your own life and in the lives of those you care about.

Chapter One

No Excuses: Take Control of Your Life Now!

⁓

Productivity is the ability to get results—results that help other people, change their lives, and help them get results as well. The great tragedy today is that people take as little schooling as they can. They take the easiest courses possible, get average grades—just enough to get through—and fail to continually upgrade their ability to get results that people will pay them for.

Here I want to give people mental and physical tools that they can use to get better results faster. As a result, they will earn more money, be promoted faster, and—best of all—feel wonderful about themselves. You shouldn't be productive just for money or to please your boss. You ought to be productive because you'll feel happy.

We want to get results for others. Many years ago, an old acquaintance, motivational teacher Earl Nightingale, said that your rewards in life will be in direct proportion to the results that you get for other people. We always get what we deserve,

---

**Your rewards in life will always be in direct proportion
to the results that you get for other people.**

---

he said: you never get more or less than you deserve. Many people's lives are ruined because they're trying to get more out than they put in. They're trying to get more than they deserve. Earl said the word *deserve* comes from the Latin *deservire*, which is derived from *servire*: *to serve*. You get what you get from serving other people in some way.

People ask me, "How can I earn more money? How can I get ahead faster?"

I say, "You must focus single-mindedly all day, every day, on serving other people better, on upgrading your knowledge and skills so that you can help people achieve their goals, fulfill their promise, overcome their obstacles, and solve their problems. You must always be thinking about serving other people." That is productivity.

Many people think that work is a punishment that you have to suffer to get through life. People who have this belief are always at the financial bottom of society. They earn less than others, they are often unemployed, and they are very seldom promoted. The fact is that work is what fulfills us as individuals. Our job is to find the kind of work that we most like.

Many years ago, Napoleon Hill, author of *Think and Grow Rich*, said that if you find a job you love, you'll never work another day in your life. One of your most important responsibilities is to dream big dreams and do what you love to do. This is your responsibility.

When I was an executive, I had people come to me and say, "I'm thirty-five years old. I'm not going anywhere in my life. Can you help me? Can you guide me? Can you take me into your company and give me the training and support I need to do good work and get paid?"

I'd say, "Nobody can do this for you but you." It's like being a good parent. You can't farm it out. It's only you—face-to-face, head-to-head, knee-to-knee, heart-to-heart with the members of your family—who can be a good husband or a good parent. There's no other way to do it.

Therefore your job is to find something that you enjoy doing. If you could do anything that you wanted for work in the whole world, what would it be, and how would it be different from what you're doing today? If you are not now doing what you love to do, then you have to pull back and say, "If I don't love this, what *would* I love?"

If you are not doing what you love, ask yourself:
"If I don't love this, what *would* I love?"

Many people say, "I don't love my work right now, so I should find something else." No, wait. You only love your work, you're only productive at your work, when you're doing something that you're good at. Therefore your job is to become very good at what you do. Never give up what you're doing just because you're mediocre, because sometimes just one step further you will break through and you will do your work well. Suddenly all the lights go on, and you feel happy and can hardly wait to get to work.

Successful people are always self-disciplined. They discipline themselves to start early, work harder, stay later, get more done. You have to discipline them *not* to work, to do things that other people think are fun, because work is their way of fulfilling themselves. Their work, their ability to produce results, is what makes them feel happy about being alive.

Let me share a little about my own experience. When I started off in sales, I would get up at 6:00 or 6:30 in the morning, and I would go to work at 7:00 or 7:30. I would knock on doors. I didn't have a car, so I would have to take a bus into the city, and I'd knock on doors hour after hour. In the evenings, I would go out and knock on doors in the neighborhoods, in the apartments, and in the homes.

I didn't make my first sale, and it was a small sale, until thirty days after I started selling. After that, I made one or two sales a week. I didn't earn very much, and I struggled. I found that when you are not very good at what you do, you associate with other people who aren't very good either. Pretty soon you develop a worldview that this is the way it is. Nobody does well, sales are hard, and it will only be hard.

Then one day I asked a successful salesperson what advice he could give me. He was earning ten times as much as anybody else in our company. He was earning more, and he didn't even seem to be working very hard. He'd start at 9:00 in the morning, and he'd quit at 5:00 or 5:30. He went to nice restaurants, and he had a pocket full of money, and here I was, working away, slogging, and taking the bus.

"Well," he said, "have you ever read any books on selling?"

Now I'm a reader; I like to read. I said, "Are there books on selling?"

**Productive people are self-disciplined.
They discipline themselves to: start earlier, work harder,
stay later, and get more done than others.**

"Yes," he said, "some of the best salespeople in the world have written some great books."

I couldn't believe it. I went down to the bookstore immediately. There were dozens and dozens of books on sales that had been written by top salespeople, who had gone from rags to riches. I bought my first book on selling.

I clutched it to me. I took it home. It was called *Making Sales Faster*, or something like that. I took it home, and I read it. Here was a man with thirty years of experience, who'd worked his way up into senior management, where he recruited and trained and managed large sales forces, and he was telling me how to do it.

Where do you start? Whom do you contact? How do you contact them? What do you say when you meet with them? How do you follow up? How do you position yourself against your competition, and so on?

I couldn't believe it. I felt I'd died and gone to heaven. I began to read and read, and my sales started to go up. I started to become happier. I started to make more money, and people started to look at me as if I were smoking something or drinking some kind of elixir.

Then I said to myself, "Of all the sales skills that I would need to be more successful, what would be the most important?" It's closing the sale.

I was no longer afraid to knock on doors and talk to people. Sometimes I talked too much, and too fast. I learned later when you meet a customer, you don't talk and talk. You ask questions, and you listen carefully to the answers. You look for ways of helping this customer improve the quality of their life or work.

You keep asking questions, and then you show that your product or service would be ideal for this customer. You show how you can help your customer get better results, be more productive, or get more out of life and more income out of their work or business.

I realized, however, that closing the sales was the problem. I would get right to the final point, and I'd just be paralyzed. I was like a deer in the headlights.

So I said, "All right. I'm going to learn about closing sales." I went down to the bookstore, and I looked at every book I could on how to close a sale. I took these books home, and I studied hour after hour in the evenings and mornings and weekends about how to close a sale.

Within a month, my income had gone up four or five times. Within a year, it had gone up ten times, because I learned a variety of ways to ask for the order. Not one of these ways was manipulative or high-pressure or grinding the person down. They were just helpful, intelligent ways of asking questions to help the person make a buying decision.

I then began to teach other people what I had learned, and their sales went up and up and up. Pretty soon, I was a sales manager, and I began to recruit other salespeople. I taught them the basic sales process and showed them how to ask for the order. I have made more people into millionaires over the years by helping them to sell well and then ask for the order than maybe anybody else in history. My books are now in thirty or forty languages. They've been used by millions of salespeople. At the audio company Nightingale-Conant, my friend Vic Conant told me that they had done a survey and found that more people had become millionaires using my materials in selling than any other sales influence. I'm not surprised, because it made me a millionaire as well.

So it will work for you. Here's another thing: *all sales skills are learnable.* People at the top of their field in sales will tell you that when they started off, they were terrible. They couldn't sell. They starved. They lived out of their cars, or they slept on the floor of their friends' apartments.

Then they learned the skill. Any skill that anyone else has learned, you can learn as well. This is one of the most wonderful things about productivity: you have the ability to be five and ten times as productive as you are today, and the skills are very simple and straightforward. How do we know? Because you are surrounded by people who are earning vastly more than you are. When they started off, they were earning vastly *less* than you are, but they learned some of the skills that I'll talk about in this book. They learned these skills, and they practiced them over and over.

Any skills that anyone else has learned, you can learn as well.

Everything at the beginning is difficult, but when you work at it, it becomes easy and automatic. We will make high productivity easy and automatic.

Today, if you offered me $1,000 an hour to work for you, I would have to decline. I'd say, "I'm sorry. I book my time out for much more than that. I would like to help you, but I just don't work at that rate." At one time, my first job paid $1.12 an hour. If you had offered me $5 an hour, I would have asked, "Who do I have to kill to get $5 an hour?"

Today I wouldn't accept $1,000. I know countless people for whom $1,000 an hour is of no interest because they earn so much more. But when they started, they started with nothing; they started off at the bottom.

The most important thing is to make a decision. Make a decision about how much money you want to earn. Make a decision about what you're going to have to do to earn that money. Make a decision about what skill you're going to have to master. Make a decision about how you're going to organize your time and your life in order to get the results that will cause people to happily pay you the kind of money that you want to earn.

Make four key decisions to turbo-charge your productivity

1. How much money you want to earn.
2. What you are going to do to earn it.
3. What skills you are going to have to master to earn it. Deliberately practice one skill at a time.
4. How to organize your time and your life to earn it.

Angela Duckworth's book *Grit* says the most important quality of successful people is that they have determination. No matter how many disappointments they have, they just pick themselves up, and they just keep working. They just keep pushing forward every hour of every day. No matter how many times they're set back, they bounce back. Similarly, successful people select skills that they need to master, and they deliberately practice those skills all the time. One of the success secrets of self-made millionaires and billionaires is that they started developing one skill at a time.

Furthermore, every one of these millionaires gets up early in the morning. You'll find it repeated over and over again: successful people get up at 5:00 or 6:00 in the morning. The average self-made millionaire gets up before 6:00 a.m.

I made that decision years ago. I set my mental clock, so I can see my clock from my bed. When it gets to be five minutes to 6:00, I get up. I get up and get moving, almost as if the house is on fire. I get up, I start moving, and I start the day with physical exercise. Because I live in the San Diego area, most of the year I can get up, go downstairs, throw myself in the pool, and thrash back and forth ten or twenty times.

When I was buying this house years ago, I wanted a house that had a ten-stroke pool. I looked at a lot of houses. I finally found this one, and I paced off the pool from corner to corner: ten strokes.

So I go in and do fifty strokes, five laps back and forth. When you've done fifty strokes, you are wide awake. Less than twenty minutes have passed, and you are charged for the entire day.

Then wealthy people study for sixty to ninety minutes. They're conscientious about studying all the time. They're always reading. Who do you think buys and reads all these books? It's not poor people.

If you go into a rich person's house, you see books everywhere. I was talking to a successful real estate agent who sold expensive homes in expensive neighborhoods. He said when he would show a couple a house, the woman would ask where the living room is and where the kitchen is, and the man would ask where the den is, where the study is, and where the office is. He found that when wealthy people bought homes, they needed places for their books because they had so many. They had to have a library. One of the most attractive things you could do is put in a library, rows and rows empty for books, because rich people would be highly attracted to that.

My late friend, the entrepreneurial speaker Jim Rohn, once said if you go into the homes of rich people, you see books everywhere. When you go into the homes of poor people, you see the biggest television that they can afford, and no books. They just don't read.

Many wealthy people create a television room. I have a good friend, author Robert Allen, who has a lovely home. He has a complete theater for watching TV. But you actually have to get up and go from one side of his house to the other and down into the theater to watch it. He does that to make it harder to mindlessly watch TV.

Don't make it so easy that you can just click it on when you come home at night, and when you get up in the morning, and during the weekends. The average wealthy person watches TV maybe an hour to an hour and a half a day. By comparison, the average poor person watches TV anywhere from five to seven hours a day.

What do these people do if they're not watching television? They spend time with their families. They talk to their spouses. They talk to their kids. Kids develop their personalities, their self-esteem, and their self-confidence by the amount of time their parents spend talking to them, asking questions, and listening to them talk. It's absolutely essential.

In the best marriages, you come home at night—they call this the *hour of power*—and you talk to your spouse. You don't say, "Where's the remote control?" and run off and watch television for the rest of the night.

These are some habits of wealthy people: they're continually building relationships with their family, and they're learning all the time. They read all the time.

My wife and I have four children. All of our kids have stacks of books and bookcases and libraries. They read all the time. Sometimes it seems that they've read more than I have, and I'm a big reader. I read no less than three hours a day and sometimes more.

These are some of the habits of successful people. If you want to be successful, if you want to be rich, do what rich people do. If you want to be poor, do what poor people do.

Habits of self-made millionaires and billionaires:

- Deliberately practice and develop one skill at a time
- Get up early in the morning
- Study their profession for 60 to 90 minutes a day
- Minimize TV watching and focus on developing relationships

Napoleon Hill wrote the most successful book on wealth building in history: *Think and Grow Rich*. He created more millionaires than perhaps any other writer in history. They called him the millionaire maker, and that was his goal, by the way. His goal was to be known as the millionaire maker. He did twenty-two years of research interviewing self-made multimillionaires to find out how they became rich. He put it all into a system. People simply picked the system up, like a recipe in a kitchen, and they followed the recipe until they had mastered it.

I'm not a good cook, but I can cook certain dishes really well. Someone asked me recently why I'm so good at these dishes. It's because of practice; I practiced them over and over again. The first time I made them, they didn't taste good at all, but after a few weeks or months, I reached the point where not only did they taste really good, but I could whip them up without even thinking about it. I can make these dishes automatically, and they are absolutely delicious just from practice.

At one time, I had no skill in cooking at all, and now I do. At one time, I had no skill in selling, and now I do. I have taught more than two million people in eighty-three countries how to sell.

People tell me, "You changed my life. You made me rich. I didn't realize that selling was a skill you could master. I thought you just went out, knocked on doors, and hoped you'd talk to someone who needed your product. I didn't realize that it was a science, it was an art, it was a practice."

Napoleon Hill kept up his research, and he wrote another book called *The Master Key to Riches*. He wrote many books, but those were the two great ones. *The Master Key to Riches* goes on for about 250 pages, and it ends with a final line in the final paragraph of the final chapter: "The master key to riches is self-discipline."

People succeed because they're highly disciplined. I have written one of the best-selling books in the world on this subject. It's called *No Excuses: The Power of Self-Discipline.* All over the world, people line up with copies of the book in their language for me to autograph.

I've studied this subject exhaustively, and I've found that if you have self-discipline, you can accomplish almost anything. If you don't, you can accomplish nothing. People accomplish extraordinary things even though they're surrounded by distractions and gadgets by disciplining themselves to leave these things off.

One key to success in life today is to leave electronic devices off. If they're on, turn them off. If you must check your email, check it two times or three times a day. Turn it on, check it, get off, and turn it off, because it is simply too distracting. When your email dings, you have no power to resist jumping to see what's there. It's like a knee-jerk reaction. They call it the *slot-machine effect.* People are sitting there, the email slot machine beeps, and they think, "Ah, what did I win? I must have won something." They immediately turn to their computer to check their email. If it's a piece of junk, they say, "Oh, heck." They send the email to someone else, so they ring somebody else's bell. It goes back and forth—ring, bing, ring, bing.

It takes the average person seventeen minutes to get back to work after being distracted by an email or a text message.

**Resist the *Slot Machine Effect,* and minimize
use electronic devices as much as possible.**

Some take more, some less; some never get back to work. They get distracted at 11:00 in the morning, and they take care of the email. Now it's 11:17, and they say, "Jeez, it's almost lunchtime. There's no point in getting back to the job. I'll do it after lunch." They go looking for someone they can go to lunch with. They go out for lunch, and they come back, and they decide, "It's time to rebuild all my relationships with my coworkers," so they go around talking and phoning and sending emails.

So just leave those devices off. Have the discipline to turn them off.

Email: Work Dessert

Today many people have a very difficult time managing their email. Some have thousands of emails in their inbox. Personally, I clear out my email every day first thing, and then I work on my tasks all day long.

One technique is discipline yourself to perform your most important task first thing in the morning, before anything else, and then reward yourself for completing this task by checking your email. Checking your email is kind of like a work dessert. People love to do it.

Keep your finger on the delete button. Do not be controlled by people who send you miscellaneous emails. I get them every day; everybody does. They're very tempting. They have attractive lines, potential benefits, and everything else. What you do is just delete, delete, delete. Don't allow yourself to be drawn in.

Keys to managing e-mail:

- It takes the average person 17 minutes to get back to work after being distracted by an e-mail or text message.
- Make checking e-mail a "work dessert": Only check e-mail as a reward to yourself after completing your most important tasks.
- Keep your finger on the delete button.
- Don't be drawn in by miscellaneous e-mails.
- Check e-mail 2–3 times per day.
- File important e-mails, delete the rest, and get back to important tasks.

A few years ago, a friend of mine, Julie Morgenstern, wrote a great book: *Never Check Email in the Morning.* Another friend of mine, Dianna Booher, wrote *Get Over Email Overload.* It shows you how to manage email so that it's a servant to you, and not a master.

There are a lot of little tricks. I've mentioned a couple of them. People follow these rules, and as a result emails are nothing to them. They check them two or three times a day. They know exactly how to deal with them. They file them if necessary. They complete them if necessary and get on with the rest of their work.

Again, discipline is everything. Elbert Hubbard, one of the greatest American thinkers of the last century, said, "Self-discipline is the key to success." He said, "Self-discipline is the ability to make yourself do what you should do, when you should do it, whether you feel like it or not."

Note: *whether you feel like it or not.* Anybody can do anything if they feel like it. They can eat delicious food, they can drink a delicious drink. They can listen to music. They can chat with their friends. They can do things that are fun and easy rather than things that are hard and worthwhile.

Your job is to practice self-discipline. Every act of self-discipline requires persistence, and every act of persistence builds your self-esteem. It makes you feel stronger and happy about yourself. Psychologists call this a *sense of control.* You only feel happy when you feel you are in charge of your life—when you have control over your life and your work.

If you make a decision to start and complete a task, it requires discipline to get started, and it requires persistence to continue. After you have completed that task, you feel wonderful about yourself.

A habit is taking an action, getting positive feedback from the action, and taking that action again. You do that action repeatedly until it becomes easy and automatic for you. The starting point of developing self-discipline is to develop the positive habit of starting and completing your task.

Another thing that has been helpful to me is to write things down. Successful people that I know always have something to write on—a small writing pad, or a large one. They carry it with them.

One example is Vic Conant. Everywhere he went, he had his notepad with him. As soon as you started talking, he would open it up, and listen to you. He would listen to waiters; he would listen to his secretary; he would listen to anybody. He'd write down notes whenever you said something that might have value in it. He became one of the most successful businesspeople in America, and one of the most formidable influences in the world in audio recording and sales. He got there by practicing self-discipline.

Time Management

Productivity also requires planning and organizing. This means working all the time you work—an idea that is alien to most people.

Most people do not really get to work until about 11:00 a.m. When they come to work, the first thing they do is meet and greet their friends. "How are you doing? Did you see this on the television? What do you think about this and that?" Finally, about 11:00, they realize, "Jeez, it's almost lunchtime. I'd better do some work."

They do some work, and then they go for lunch. They don't get to work again until about 3:00. Then it's about 3:30 or 4:00: "Well, there's no point getting started with anything today." So they quit working.

Have you ever noticed that when you're going home after work at 4:30, the streets are clogged? These people have not gotten off work yet. How is that they're there? They're still supposed to be working, so how come they're on the road?

I did not graduate from high school. I finished school in the half of the class that makes the top half possible. The only job that I could get was washing dishes in the back of a small hotel. After that, I went on to washing cars and then to washing floors with a janitorial service. I thought washing was going to be my future. I slept in my car. I slept on the floors of friends' one-room apartments. I slept in the basement of my parents' house, and they didn't want me around.

Then I began asking why some people are more successful than others, and I began searching. I read that Aristotle was the greatest philosopher in history and that he had some of the most important insights into success.

Aristotle said that all human beings are creatures of habit. Everything that you do or don't do is a result of habits that you have developed early in life. The role of parenting is to raise children with good habits. Raise them with good habits, and they will have good character.

Which brings us back to our present subject: you are where you are and what you are because of your habits. My friend, motivational speaker Ed Foreman, used to say, "Form good habits, and make them your masters rather than allowing bad habits to form you and undermine your character." Therefore your major goal in life is to develop positive habits.

When I first started studying personal success, I found that it's all about new habit development, which takes about twenty-one days of repetition. This is not entirely true, because sometimes you can develop a habit at once; something happens that changes your thinking forever. With other habits, such as quitting smoking or changing your diet to lose weight, it's a longer process. In most cases, it takes steady repetition, over and over, and at a certain point the habit will lock in.

One of the most important habits is to work all the time you work. When we're growing up, we go to school, which we associate with playing with our friends. We go to kindergarten or first grade. At first we're a little afraid, but then we find that

"Form good habits and make them your masters rather than allowing bad habits to form you and undermine your character." —Ed Foreman

this is where our friends are, so we play with our friends. We look forward to school as our primary play place in life.

Then we grow up, and we play in different ways. We play grownup games, and we go to sports; everything is playing with our friends. We do enough schoolwork so that we don't get thrown out and we're allowed to keep coming there, but basically it's playtime.

When we get out of school and get our first job, we're nervous and fearful again. The first day of our first job is often one of the most terrifying days of all. We go to work, and we're nervous, and we look around. We see a lot of people our own age, and they're all fairly friendly. What do you do when you associate with people your own age? Just like in school, you play.

Work becomes our primary play place. We go to work, and as a result of habit, we play with our friends. We have to do a certain amount of work, or they won't let you come back; they'll fire you, and you won't have a job. So you do as much work as you need to do so you can go there and play with your friends. You look forward to seeing your friends, you look forward to going out after work, and you look forward to weekends.

The most important thing is to develop the habit of working all the time you work. Just repeat to yourself that the workplace is not a play place; it is a workplace. When you walk in the door at 8:30 or before, your job is to hit it, start working, and work all day long.

If somebody wants to talk to you, say, "I'd love to talk to you, but let's talk after work. Let's talk at lunchtime." Or "I'd love to talk to you right now, but I have work I have to get done as quickly as possible. My boss is expecting the work."

As it happens, nobody will stop you from doing your work. They'll say, "OK, I'll talk to you later." Eventually they will leave you alone, because you're no fun; you don't want to play at work.

Your job is to work all the time you work.

Here's another important habit that you can develop. It is to *complete your tasks*. This is the key to high productivity. Work all the time you work, and complete your tasks. Once you start on a task, put your head down and hit it. Work at that task until it's done.

A major source of stress in our society today is that we're overwhelmed with work that we haven't gotten done. So set priorities: "If I could only complete one task a day, what one task would have the greatest positive effect on my career, would help my company or my business the most?" Whatever it is, pick that one task, start on it, and work on it until it's complete.

Now here's a wonderful discovery: task completion increases self-esteem and self-confidence. It earns you the respect and admiration of other people. It is the key to high income and to greater opportunities and more jobs and responsibilities. Everything in the world of work is task completion. It's not doing the work. It's finishing the work.

Always think in terms of task completion. It's very much like running a race and coming in first. If you run a race and come in first, what do they call you? The winner. That's right.

Get a reputation so people will say "If you want the job done give it to her. She'll get it done, and she'll get it done quickly and well."

When you complete a task, you feel like the winner. Nobody else has to be competing with you. The very completion makes you feel like a winner. Your self-esteem goes up. Your energy goes up. You feel happy. People around you—especially the people who can most affect your career—smile at you and like you. Behind your back, they say, "If you want to get something done, ask him, because you give him a job, and he'll do it. He will hammer and hammer. He will stay late, come in early, and work weekends, but he will do the job."

When I started working, I developed this habit of completing my tasks. Sometimes I would work late at night and all weekend long. Once I was working for a big boss in a fast-growing company with 200 businesses under its umbrella. He gave me a job to do on a Friday. He said, "This is important to me. I'd appreciate it if you would do this assessment and write it up."

I said, "OK." This was Friday afternoon, and I stayed until about 8:00 that night. I called my wife and told her I'd be home late. Then I worked all Saturday and all Sunday. I came in Monday morning, and I had the whole report all typed up.

When he came in later, which he almost always did at 10:00, the report was waiting on his desk. He came to my office and said, "This is remarkable. I really appreciate your getting it done. It wasn't really that important right away—a week or two would have been fine—but thank you very much for doing it."

The report was an analysis of a business opportunity that involved many millions of dollars. The head of the bank called him later that day and said, "Look, I hate to put you under any pressure, but I actually need that report right away in order to approve the loan for your company." The loan was $50 million.

"As a matter of fact," my boss said, "I have the whole analysis complete. I'll send it right over to you." He did, and they approved the loan. It had a major impact on the company. He came to me and told me what had happened. Again he told me how much he appreciated it and walked away. He wasn't a talkative man, but from that time on, whenever there was something that needed to be done and done quickly, he gave it to me.

I went from a small office to a bigger office to the second-biggest office in the company. I went from working by myself late into the night to having a staff that fulfilled my responsibilities. I went from working on my little job to having three divisions of the company under my control. I went from struggling to earning more than I ever earned in my life.

Years later, I hired the controller of that company to run my businesses. He said, "By the way, that boss paid you more in salaries, bonuses, and commissions than he ever paid anybody in his career." He had hundreds of people working for him over the course of his career. He would always say to the accounting staff, "If there's something that you need to get done, give it to Brian, because he'll do it quickly, and he'll do it well."

This is your key to success, to high productivity, to high income, to opportunity, and to feeling wonderful about yourself and being respected by everyone around you: do your work, and do it quickly and well.

Work all the time you work, finish your tasks, and get them done. Don't worry if it's too soon or too early. Get a reputation so that people will say, "If you want the job done, give it to her. She'll get it done, and she'll get it done quickly and well."

What is your reputation now? How is your reputation different from other people in your company? Do people say about you that if you want it done quickly and well, give it to you rather than to anybody else?

Think about that, because what determines your future more than anything else is what people say about you and your work when you're not there.

The Meaning of Success

Let me go back to the question that changed my life when I was coming out of my teens: why are some people more successful than others? Then another question immediately came up: what is success? Is success earning a lot of money?

No. Success is living your life the way that you want to live your life. It's doing the things that you want to do. It's doing the work that you enjoy, and doing that work with people you enjoy and respect.

Success, more than anything else, is freedom. Freedom, to me, is the most important joy of life—to feel completely free, to be who you are, do what you want, and take other jobs.

Today we talk about the economic boom. There are supposed to be about seven million jobs open in America today, more than in any other country in the world. Companies large and small have openings for which they need people, but no matter how much they want to pay, they can't find people who will get the job done. So they advertise and promote, they hire and train, and then they fire these people and get someone else.

If you want to have complete freedom to feel wonderful about yourself and your life, become known as the person who produces results. If they give you a job to do, do it, and do it quickly and well. You don't grumble, you don't complain, and you don't say you're really busy or overwhelmed.

I have never turned down a task in my life. When I was young and poor, I didn't know that this was really important. For me, it was an opportunity to be successful. They opened a door for me. My boss said, "Here's the door; run through it," and I did.

The average people in my company resented me. They talked about me behind my back. They badmouthed me behind my back because I was working all the time, while they would come in, get together for coffee, and go for lunch. They would sit and chat, and they'd come back. Then they'd go out for drinks at the end of the day. But I was working all the time.

I read a review of the autobiography of baseball player Pete Rose. They used to call him Pete Hustle, because that was his philosophy. His father taught him to move fast when the ball moved. I met him once, and he was a great guy. Everybody liked him because he was positive, he was optimistic, and he was a hustler. He would run faster, and he would be more determined and more persistent than anybody. He became one of the best players in American baseball history. He'd be in the Hall of Fame if he hadn't had certain problems during his career.

So I always think of him as Pete Hustle—the Hustler. That's what you should be. Get a reputation for being a hustler. If someone wants something done and done well and done quickly, they give it to you, and door after door will opens for you.

When I left the big boss—he had sold his company for $850 million, and he retired to a smaller business operation—the phone rang. I was immediately hired by the second richest person in Western Canada, another billionaire who called me and said, "Can you come and work for me?"

"Sure," I said, because I saw an opportunity there.

"How much are you earning from the big boss?" he asked "How much is he paying you?" I told him. He said, "I'll pay you triple. When can you start?"

So I went back and had a talk with the big boss, and told him that it was time for me to move on, and I went to work with this gentleman. He put me immediately in charge of a $265 million division of the company.

Having a reputation for getting things done quickly transformed my life. That's one of the most important habits that you can develop. Develop good habits, and develop them by practice. When you're developing a new habit, never allow an exception. Never give yourself an excuse or let yourself off the hook on the grounds that you're tired and worked really hard this week and have too many things to do.

No excuses. That's the title of my book, the best-selling book on this subject in the world today: *No Excuses: The Power of Self-Discipline.*

Tips for Developing Successful Habits

1. Developing new habits takes steady repetition of a behavior, over and over, until the new habit locks in.
2. Develop the habit of *"working" all the time you are at work.*
3. Develop the habit of *completing all of your tasks.*
4. Developing habits requires total personal responsibility for results—no excuses.

Chapter Two

Master the Productivity Mindset

feel it's important not to just give people techniques and strategies, but to give them a deeper understanding of the psychology that underlies the discipline in question, be it sales, leadership, negotiation, persuasion, or achievement.

Why? Let me go back to a simple statement that goes back to Ralph Waldo Emerson and Earl Nightingale: *you become what you think about most of the time.* Your outer world is an expression of your inner world. You don't get what you want in life. You get what you expect. The law of attraction says you attract into your life the people and circumstances that are in harmony with your dominant thoughts.

The most wonderful thing in the world is that the only thing over which you have complete control are the thoughts that you

Your outer world is an expression of your inner world.

think. The more you think positive thoughts about yourself and your possibilities, the more creative you are.

Each person has not only a conscious mind but a subconscious mind as well. The subconscious mind is very much misunderstood. Basically it's a huge mental library that stores every experience you've ever had in your life and makes that information available to you when you need it.

Each person also has a superconscious mind. This superconscious mind has been talked about, possibly, for 4,000 years. This is your ability to communicate with a great mind in the universe to which all people can turn. It's almost like a great mind that surrounds you at all time. Just as we can tune into the Internet today, we can turn into the superconscious mind. It will bring us everything we want if we want it long enough and hard enough and work toward it in the proper way.

I find that all successful people are aware that this great mind exists. Last week I spoke to a very successful woman, and I said, "Of course you have heard about the superconscious mind."

"Absolutely," she said.

If you feed this superconscious mind with very clear thoughts, it will bring you everything that you want and need at exactly the right time for you. If you want to be happy, the key is to tap into your superconscious mind.

This takes me back to a major turning point in my life, which was my discovery of the role of self-esteem. Self-esteem is best described as how much you like yourself, how much you respect yourself, how much you consider yourself to be a valuable and worthwhile person. Your self-esteem determines virtually everything that happens to you in life. Furthermore,

**Self-esteem is how much you like yourself,
respect yourself and consider yourself a
valuable and worthwhile person.**

everything that happens either increases or decreases your self-esteem. Nothing in life is neutral.

I learned this about self-esteem before my first child was born. I sat down with my wife. We decided that our number one goal was to raise our children with high self-esteem and high levels of self-confidence. Everything we have done has focused on that. We have deliberately never criticized them, never punished them, never done anything that would diminish their self-esteem or their self-confidence.

My first child, my guinea pig, was my daughter Christina. Then my son, Michael, and then my son David, and my daughter Catherine. I've repeated this to them over and over again. As they say in the Wild West, "Never is heard a discouraging word." My children have never been criticized or encouraged to have self-limiting beliefs, because I tell them they are really excellent, and they can do anything they put their mind to.

Moreover, 95 percent of your emotions are determined by how you talk to yourself most of the time. The very best words that you can possibly use, the blanket affirmation, is, "I like myself. I like myself. I like myself." The more you like yourself, the better you do everything you apply your mind to, the more confidence you have, the happier you are, and the more energy you have. Say, "I like myself. I like myself. I like myself."

Recently I was contacted by a young man who had just become the general manager of a fast-growing technical company, and he said, "I have to tell you my story. You won't believe it, but I'm going to send it to you on your iPhone. I'm just going to record a message to you," and he did.

He had started off selling cell phones in a kiosk in a mall. He had been working for a month, but he hadn't sold a single phone. He kept calling on people who said, "I'm not interested. I don't want it. I don't need it. I have a phone." He was really down on himself. He was in despair.

He went to the bookstore in the mall and came across a book of mine. It was called *The Psychology of Selling* (which is a detailed explanation of how your thinking determines your sales). He read it, and he was especially struck by the statement "I like myself."

The next day, he stopped in the parking lot. He took out the book, turned to that page, and started repeating over and over, "I like myself. I like myself." He saw people walking past the car while he was there talking to himself very enthusiastically. They were pointing to him, and he was laughing and saying, "I like myself. I like myself."

Then he got up and went into the mall. From that moment on, he became a selling machine. He sold and sold and sold. Within a month, he was the top salesman in the company. Within two months, he was a supervisor. Within three months, he was an executive. Within four months, he started his own business. Every day, he got himself cranked up with "I like myself. I like myself."

It's the same thing with you. The most powerful words that you can say to yourself are "I like myself" over and over. Then you say, "I can do it. I can do it. I can do it." over and over.

If you want to raise happy, healthy, self-confident children, tell them constantly, "You can do it. You can do it. You can do anything you put your mind to. There's nothing you cannot do if you really want to." Remember, you have the greatest influence in the world over the people who look up to you: your children, your spouse, your employees, your friends. Whenever you tell them, "You can do it. You can do anything you put your mind to," they believe you, and pretty soon that becomes a habit of belief for them.

The more you believe yourself to be a highly productive person, starting and finishing your tasks every day, the happier you'll feel, the more energy you'll have, the more you'll like and respect yourself, and the more motivated you'll be to come in a little earlier, work a little harder, and stay a little later. You'll become motivated to study and learn and become better at the most important things to you, your boss, and your company. You'll become a learning machine. You can hardly wait to learn new things that make you more capable of doing more and better work and doing it faster for the people who expect it from you and look up to you.

Many people behave in the opposite way. They denigrate themselves. They sabotage themselves with mental chatter that reinforces the belief that they aren't productive.

The greatest limitation on your success—the two things that hold you back more than anything else—are the fear of failure, the fear that you won't do it well, and the fear of rejection, the fear that other people will dislike you and criticize you. Those are the two fears that you have to overcome more than anything else. Wonderfully, the more you say, "I like myself," and "I can do it," the smaller those fears become; they diminish and

---

**The greatest limitation on your success are the
fear of failure and the *fear of rejection*.**

---

diminish until they don't exist at all. If they do come into your mind, you immediately shoo them out.

With self-limiting beliefs, you believe you are limited in some way. You are limited in a talent, in a skill. You're not good enough. You are not attractive enough. You're not skilled enough. The biggest single problem that human beings have is summarized in the words, "I'm not good enough. Others are better than me."

So I tell my students that they are as good or better as anyone they will ever meet. When you repeat over and over again, "I like myself," and "I can do it," eventually you start to believe it. Your negative, self-limiting beliefs diminish.

So tell yourself those things over and over again. Tell the most important people in your life, "You can do it, and you are really good at what you do. You are really excellent."

When my children were four years or five years old, they'd come home from school with their first little pictures, and they'd show them to me. I would make a fuss over those pictures. I'd say, "You did this? You did this by yourself? Who helped you? Who did this for you? Somebody must have done it for you?"

"No, no," they'd say. "I did it all by myself."

I'd say, "This is incredible. I can't believe it." I'd call my wife, "Barbara, you have to see this. You're not going to believe it. Look at this. Christina did this all by herself. This is amazing." We would the picture up on the mirror or on the kitchen refrigerator, and we would make a big fuss.

Even when they got a poor grade, we'd say, "That's just temporary. You're going to get a better grade next time, aren't you?"

They'd say, "Yes, I am."

"Great, no problem. That's because you're so smart."

You can do the same thing with the members of your family.

As I said at the beginning of this chapter, you become what you think about most of the time. You become what you say most of the time. You also become what you tell other people most of the time. So when you tell other people positive things, that message reflects back like a boomerang on you. You feel positive, you feel happier, and you feel stronger, and your self-esteem goes up as well. You have tremendous power with the words that you use.

You also become what you teach. Earlier I mentioned Pete Rose. Pete Rose is famous because his father taught him to play baseball from the age of four. Who is the most respected golfer in the world today? Probably Tiger Woods. Tiger Woods was playing golf with his father by the age of four. His father gave him guidance and instruction and praise and encouragement from the age of four, and he beat his father at golf by the age of six. How do you feel when you're a child and you actually beat your father, who is the great golfer in your family? Tiger Woods went on to become one of the most respected golfers in history.

Remember, everything that you say and everything that you project out from yourself bounces back, so always say things about yourself that you want to be true. Never say anything about yourself that you do not want to be true. Never say that you're late or you're disorganized or you forget things. Always talk about yourself the way you want to be in the future.

The Essentials of self-talk and affirmations:

- Ninety-five percent of your emotions are based on how you talk to yourself most of the time.
- The very best words you can say to yourself is the blanket affirmation, "I like myself."
- If you want to raise happy, self-confident children, tell them constantly: "You can do it. You can do anything you put your mind to."
- Most people sabotage themselves with mental chatter that reinforces the idea that they aren't productive.
- Never say anything about yourself, that you do not want to be true.
- When you positively influence others by telling others positive things, the message reflects back like a boomerang on you.

Productivity and Authenticity

Some people think that if you work hard all the time, stay focused, do your job, and complete your tasks, you will lose your spontaneity and authenticity. This is simply not true. When you start and complete your tasks every time, you start to feel happier and happier about yourself. You start to feel happy about getting the job done and getting the job done on time.

I encourage you to write down a plan and work on it every single day until it becomes natural for you. It becomes spontaneous for you to get the job done, and you become natural and spontaneous with others.

**Write down a plan and work on it every day
until it becomes a natural and spontaneous
way of acting—to get the job done.**

As I've said, many people waste most of their time at work. It is estimated that about 50 percent of time at work is wasted on nonproductive tasks and activities. Only about 50 percent is spent actually working, and of those tasks, many are of low value or no value at all.

So make it natural for yourself to complete your work, because then you'll be happy all the time. Offer to help other people a little bit to get started, and do their work. Remember, most people today are functioning far, far below their potential level of productivity.

The 80/20 rule kicks in. The 80/20 rule is a terrible master. It says that only 20 percent of the people can earn 80 percent of the money. If you're in the bottom 80 percent, you'll always be in debt, you'll always worry about money, you'll never be respected by other people, except other people in the bottom 80 percent. And those are not people whose respect is valuable, because it's very shallow, and it goes quickly. You want to be respected by the top 20 percent.

A friend of mine became the top salesman in his company nationally. He said that when he started off working, he was at the bottom of the deck, and he hung around with the other low-level salespeople. They came into the office, they wasted time, they read the paper, and they talked and went out for lunch.

Then my friend noticed something that changed his life: out of thirty or forty salespeople in the company, there were about half a dozen that were really good. These salespeople hung out with each other, and they didn't spend any time with the poor performers. So he said, "If I'm going to be a top performer, I should associate with the top performers. How could I do that? I'll ask them for advice."

So he went to one of the top performers and said, "Look, I want to be successful like you. How do you organize your time so that you're much more productive than the average people?"

The other man said, "Well, I use this system," and showed him the system.

My friend said, "Thank you very much. I really appreciate it." He immediately put it into action.

This is one of the most important things I've ever learned: when you get a good idea, immediately take action on it. Don't wait until tomorrow or next week. Do it immediately. If somebody tells you a good idea, do it immediately, and go and tell them, "I did it, and it was really helpful to me. Is there anything else that you could advise me to do or not to do?"

They'll say, "Well, you might do this. I learned to always start earlier than anybody else, so you can get started on your work before the other people come in. Then you're much more likely to stay at it for the rest of the day."

"Ah. Thank you very much. That's a great idea." When people give you a piece of advice, write it down. Carry a notebook and write it down.

Then my friend started asking other people. He said, "You know, I asked Bill or Susan, and they gave me this advice. What kind of advice would you have for me, because I want to be successful like you?"

> ## To master the 80/20 Rule in your profession:
> 1. Ask for advice from the best performers in your field
> 2. Take action on that advice immediately and feed it back.

People would give him advice. "Pretty soon," he said, "they invited me to go for lunch with them or meet them for breakfast. Pretty soon I was spending all my time with the top people, and my sales went up and up.

"When I went to the big annual sales meeting, where all the top salespeople were, I did the same thing. I went around to the people who got all the prizes, and I asked them, 'How is that every year you get the prizes for the top salesperson in the country? What's your secret?'

"They'd say, 'Well, this is one thing I did. This is a book that I read, or this is something I do every single day, which really helped me.'

"They would tell me their secrets of success, and I would do them. Within a couple of years, I was one of the top salespeople in the country, and I was earning ten and twenty times what other people were earning.

"I also found that nobody else ever asked these top people. They'd been going up on the stage, getting the prizes for years, and nobody asked them afterwards what they did to get up there. I was the first person who asked these people. They would send me books in the mail, because they knew that I would read them and take action on them."

So the first thing to do is ask for advice from the best people in your field. You'll be astonished how open people are to giving you advice and feedback. Second, when they give you advice, take action on it immediately, and feed it back. Tell them what you did, and what happened.

Remember, everyone starts at the bottom, but you don't have to stay there.

True Self-Esteem

I need to talk a little bit about self-esteem. On the one hand, achievement in general is closely related to self-esteem. On the other hand, is it possible to overinflate your self-esteem when it doesn't accurately reflect your actual accomplishments? For example, research has shown that American students have higher self-esteem about their own intelligence and knowledge than certain foreign students, but the latter actually score higher on tests for those qualities.

I do not believe that people have false levels of self-esteem. What they have is conceit or arrogance. They have an inflated estimation of themselves, and it is very easily deflated. It's like a balloon. With one setback, they will turn on themselves and lose their self-confidence, because it's not true self-esteem.

There's true self-esteem. This is where you genuinely like yourself because you do a good job, and other people around you like you and respect you as well. If somebody criticizes you, you just throw it off. You don't pay any attention.

If you think you're doing a great job, but your boss takes you aside and says, "You know, your performance sucks," that's going to really hurt your self-concept and your self-esteem.

So there's true self-esteem, and there's false self-esteem. True self-esteem is based on actual accomplishment and achievement that is recognized not only by yourself but by people around you. With false self-esteem, you make it up yourself, but you don't have any foundation for it. You have not accomplished anything worthwhile or superior to the results of other people.

Having low self-esteem is the biggest problem that people have, because it's like having brakes on that hold you back and slow you down. They undermine your self-confidence and cause you to see negative things about yourself.

When you like yourself, you just laugh when somebody gives you criticism. Everybody is entitled to their own opinion. It doesn't bother you at all, because your self-esteem is genuine.

I raised my children so that they would never hear anything but positive, upbeat compliments and encouragement from their parents. That doesn't mean that we don't argue or disagree, but they have never been criticized, because destructive criticism from people whose opinion you respect is the great cancer in human personality. Destructive criticism of yourself is the worst of all.

Whenever you see an adult who has problems, you can trace it back to being destructively criticized in the first four or five years of life. If a child is constantly built up and encouraged and

---

False self-esteem is conceit or arrogance, with no actual achievement; true self-esteem is where you genuinely like yourself because you do a good job, and others around you recognize and respect that accomplishment.

---

praised at an early age, they will be strong and positive and self-confident for the rest of their life.

The great news here is that if you didn't get that foundation from your childhood, you can supply it yourself. You can become your own cheerleader. You can start talking to yourself in a positive way.

Say that punctuality is a problem of yours. It's probably because you learned it from one or both of your parents: they were late, so you were late, or your friends or classmates were late. Because you wanted to get along, you did the same thing.

Let's say you want to be punctual. You say, "All right, I am a very punctual person," yet you end up coming in late. You say, "That's not like me. I'm a very punctual person. Sometimes I drop the ball, but in the main, I'm a very punctual person. I'm on time for virtually everything. I always am looking for ways to get there earlier just in case something happens."

You talk to yourself. You become your own cheerleader. You talk to yourself the way you want to be, not the way you might happen to be at this moment. If you make a mistake, you say, "I made a mistake, but that's not me. That's just a mistake. I am actually punctual."

I'll give you an example. When my children were growing up, I knew that one of the great challenges of childhood is fear: fear of failure, fear of being not as good as other kids, and so on. They would lose their enthusiasm, and they would quit at sports or something else.

I remember saying to my son David, "I know one thing about you as your father: you never give up."

"Oh, that's not true, Dad. When I fall down or I don't do well in karate or baseball or anything, I quit."

"No, no," I said. "You may think that, but in reality, you never give up. I'm your father, and I know you better than anybody, so there are occasions when you decide to pull back, but you never give up."

At the time he was playing with a friend. They were talking about personalities, and David said to him, "Well, I know one thing about myself. I never give up." When I heard him say that, I said to myself, "Wow. That's great."

To this day, if you ask any of my children, "Are you the kind of person who gives up?" they would say, "Absolutely not; I never give up," because I've told them over and over again. I say, "You're an amazingly good person. You never give up."

It never occurs to them to give up. Do they try lots of things that don't work out? Absolutely, but they never give up. So you tell yourself, "I never give up, I never give up, I never give up." Tell your children, "You never give up. I'm so proud of you because you never give up, no matter what happens. You try lots of different things, but you never give up."

"But what about this, and what about that?"

"Ah, that wasn't right for you in the first place. You went on to find something that was even better for you. You never give up."

Remember, any time you reinforce and praise another person, it has a boomerang effect. It bounces back on you, and it raises your self-esteem and self-confidence as well.

Visualization and Affirmation

Let me go on to the power of visualization. You always perform on the outside the way you see yourself on the inside. You can create new mental pictures of yourself performing at your

---

Visualization is creating a positive mental picture of yourself.

---

best on the outside, because only you can control your mental pictures. So you create a mental picture of yourself as the best person you possibly can be.

There are a thousand methods and techniques. Let's say you want to be physically fit. You take a picture of a physically fit person in a bathing suit, and you put it on your refrigerator. Then you take a picture of yourself, and you replace that person's face with your own. Every time you go to the refrigerator, there's a picture of a person with a great body with your face on it, and your subconscious mind takes that as a photograph. It actually snaps a shot and files it. When you think about eating, when you think about exercising, when you think about weight, when you think about clothes, that picture plays over and over again.

You can also take an affirmation, like "I never give up," and write it out ten times. It's like in school, when the teachers used to make you write down the opposite of something you had done wrong: "I always come to class on time," or "I always finish my work on time." They'd make you write it down ten, twenty, fifty, or 100 times. Why? Because whatever you write down repeatedly starts to form a picture within your mind.

Every time you write down a picture of a command, you actually see the picture. You write down, "I never give up," and you'll see yourself not giving up. If you write, "I work longer and harder than anyone else," you'll see yourself working longer and harder. Pretty soon your subconscious mind accepts that as a command, and you automatically obey the command.

Certain habits enable you to develop other habits far more easily. One of them is to select a quality that you admire, and then write down that quality as a positive present-tense affirmation: "I am always punctual. I start my work first thing in the morning. I work all day long. I work all the time I work. I complete every task."

Write down an affirmation, and write it down ten times. Maybe every morning, get up, and write it down ten times until you find yourself automatically behaving that way.

Here's what will happen. When you do not start work punctually or complete your tasks, you'll feel uncomfortable; you'll feel a little mad at yourself. You'll feel motivated to get back on track.

When you've programmed yourself with the new habit, you're going to have much more time to get much more done than ever before. Then you can start another habit. You can say, "I always start and complete my tasks," or "I always treat people with warmth and respect." As you move up, you can create new habits that your earlier habits give you more time and opportunity to use.

Acting the Part

Another strategy is acting the part. Actors will wear the clothes that their character wears. They will see themselves in the exact physical situation of the character, and they'll repeat it over and over again until they actually become that person. Often, in fact, they have a hard time getting back to normal after they've shot a movie, because they have a split personality. They have lived, walked, talked, breathed, spoken that part while making the movie, which may take six months. Then they get another movie opportunity, and they have to get into that role, which is why movie actors are very neurotic.

What does this mean to you? You create the personality that you would like to be. What kind of a person would I like to be, consistent with my values, goals, and personality? For example, I wanted to be a positive, effective, encouraging father. So I visualized myself as a really good father to my children. I've had all kinds of situations with my children over the years, and I treat them the way a positive, loving, encouraging person would treat them.

Even if inside I'm angry or frustrated or disappointed, I realize that what I do and say is going to have an impact on how they think and feel about themselves in the future. So I'd better speak and act in a very positive way. That's how their self-esteem is developed.

Benchmarking against the Best

I have a speaking academy, and I bring twelve people together once every two months. For three days, I teach them intensively how to give excellent speeches.

I have downloaded well-known speeches by great actors and politicians. One of my favorites is the "I Have a Dream" speech by Martin Luther King. The best single speech of the nineteenth century is considered to be Abraham's Lincoln's "Gettysburg Address." Many children are taught that in school, so I download it and play it, so people have a picture in their mind of what a great speaker is.

There are recordings of Winston Churchill's best speeches; you play and you listen to those; sometimes you get a book and read it. It'll show how he prepared for that talk, how he wrote notes in the margin, and how he walked back and forth at home and worked with his secretary and his wife until he was thoroughly prepared to give that speech in Parliament.

In the British Parliament, when you were going to give a speech was scheduled on the docket. People would read the docket and see that at 10:40 a.m. Churchill was speaking. The word would go out up and down the halls—"Winston is up. Winston is speaking today"—and members from everywhere would go to the chamber so that they could be in their seats when Churchill spoke.

I teach my students how to speak like that, and it's astonishing. People who have never given a speech before get standing ovations the first time they speak, because they have a mental image of people standing up and cheering for them.

Essentially you want to find others that you consider to be among the most productive in your field. See if you can read an autobiographical sketch about them or their daily habits, so that you can match what you're doing against what they do.

As a young man, I learned that great leaders read about other leaders when they're growing up. They consume biographies and autobiographies, and they develop a picture of being that leader, that person who accomplished something extraordinary—military or political leaders or great scientists or great sports figures. They imagine that they are like those people. Eventually, they program themselves to think, walk, talk, and act like those people.

Becoming a Teacher

Another technique is to become a teacher. As we've seen, you become what you think about most of the time. You become what you read about most of the time. You become what you say to yourself most of the time. You also become what you teach most of the time.

So if you teach other people things that are really important to you, you start to instill those ideas into your own personality. If you teach courage, you become courageous. If you teach fastidiousness or good work habits, you develop those habits yourself.

You become what you teach, and you teach what you most want to learn. If you are really interested in a subject, you want to learn more and more about it, because deep in your subconscious and superconscious mind, you've received a message that this knowledge can be helpful to you.

A similar technique is to be a role model for others. I've worked with tens of thousands of managers over the years. When you become a manager, everyone is watching you out of the corner of their eye. They're discussing you and talking about you. They're thinking about you and talking about you at home. Even if they're not looking at you directly, they are looking and watching and taking notes. If they admire you, they will want to become like you.

One of the most wonderful things that you can do is help them by giving them books to read. Over the years, I have given books and audio programs to my staff. After years have passed, they come back to me and say, "You changed my life when you gave me that book. It changed my life forever. Now I'm a senior executive, or I have my own company, or I am earning more than I ever dreamed I would ever earn." So remember, everyone is watching you when you assume a position of authority.

Many years ago I worked in Africa with Dr. Albert Schweitzer. Schweitzer was a brilliant man. He was considered one of the greatest humanitarians of the twentieth century. I read a lot of his writing afterward. He said that you must teach men at the school of example, for they will learn at no other.

In raising children, I learned that your children are formed more by your example than by anything you say. They will ignore what you say, but they will remember what you do. At thirty-five years old, people are still being influenced by what their parents said and how they behaved.

If you want to raise happy, healthy children, love their mother, and treat her with great respect and warmth, because that's how they will grow up. I have two boys that are married now, and they both treat their wives with great affection and respect. They never argue or fight with them. They're always happy with them. They have children, and they're raising their children the same way. My daughter is married to a wonderful man, and they have three children. He treats her the way I treated her mother. My daughter was attracted to her husband at the age of fifteen because he had the qualities that I demonstrated with my wife. At a subconscious level, she wanted to have that kind of husband.

At the age of fourteen and fifteen, they met on vacation. They decided that when they grew up, they would get married.

They grew up. They finished college. They eventually moved in with each other, and then got married. It was all laid out. They were attracted to each other because that's what they saw when they were growing up.

Tips for Programming the Habit of Productivity:

- Put a picture of your desired goal on your refrigerator or mirror where you can look at it every day.
- Write out an affirmation of your goal ten times every morning right when you wake up for 30 days. Such as "I always start and complete my tasks" and "I never give up."
- Act the part of a productive person, by consciously living, acting, talking and speaking the way a productive person would.
- Benchmark yourself against the best—consume biographies and autobiographies about the productive habits, actions and philosophies of top people in your field.
- You become what you teach, so to master the goal of productivity, learn productive strategies and teach them to others.

Chapter Three

Get It Done with Crystal Clear Goal-Setting

~

As we begin to move into more specifics and strategies, it's appropriate to start with this mental strategy, which is the power of clarity. You must be absolutely clear about who you are as an individual in terms of your talents and skills and desires. As a businessperson, what are your specific goals? How much do you want to sell? How much do you want to earn? What kind of profits do you want to achieve?

You also have to be exactly clear about the benefits that your product or service will offer to your customers. You have to be clear about who your customers are, what they want and what they need, and what they're willing to pay for.

To be productive, clarity is vital. Be absolutely clear as an individual about your talents, skills, desires, and goals.

You have to be clear about your competitors. What is it that they are offering to get the customers that you want? What is it that makes them superior in the customer's mind? You have to understand how your customer sees your product in relation to your competitor's. When the customer has a choice between your product and your competitor's, why does the customer choose your competitor's? What advantages does your customer see in buying his product rather than yours? What can you do to offset those advantages?

In World War II, both the Germans and the Russians had sniper regiments. One Russian female sniper killed 387 Germans. That's more deaths than might take place in an entire battle. She was able to kill that many by shooting one shot at a time. In the Middle Eastern wars, the snipers were more dangerous and could kill more people than an entire army.

That's why I emphasize clarity. Every mistake that you will make is going to be because you are unclear about what you're trying to accomplish, unclear about your goals. Taking the time to figure this out is really important.

Albert Einstein was once asked if there were a great problem that was going to lead to the destruction of the human race, and he had one hour to solve it, how would he allocate his time? He said, "I would spend 90 percent of the time understanding the problem, and 10 percent of the time implementing the solution."

Alexander the Great was considered to be perhaps the greatest general of all time. Alexander conquered the entire known world at that time from the Mediterranean all the way through to India. He would spend days in his tent with his generals, planning each battle. They would be fighting against enemies

---

Productive problem solvers spend 90 percent of the time understanding the problem, and 10 percent of the time implementing the solution.

---

they had not fought against before. They would take the time to do the research, to do the intelligence work, to bring in prisoners and spies and find out exactly whom they were dealing with, how this enemy would come at them, and what they would have to do to win.

Alexander went against armies that were ten times larger than his, and he won every single major battle. He crossed the entire known world at that time, mountains and deserts and rivers, and was able to fight and win over and over again because he took the time to be absolutely clear about what he was dealing with and exactly what he would have to do to win.

So if you want to earn five or ten times more money than your competitors, you're going to have to have far greater clarity about what you do or can do that is worth vastly more money than your competitors.

For example, IBM started off in 1928 selling data processing card punch machines. Over time, it grew and grew. It survived the Depression quite nicely. In the sixties, they brought out a machine called the 360, which was the first major data-processing computer, and they went after the market like a storm. By 1982, they had 83 percent of the world market for computer products.

What was their key to making such incredible sales? At no time was the IBM product better or faster or cheaper than its competitors. It was always lacking in certain advantages and benefits of one competitor; it was always more expensive than another. Nevertheless, it sold most of the world's computers.

Why? Because IBM had a way of selling called the *internal rate of return*—the IRR. They said that if you buy an IBM product, it will pay for itself in a specific period of time. After that time, it will be basically cost-free; from then on, when you use the product, it will increase your profits. You'll actually make more money than you would have if you did not have this machine in place. They proved exactly how much you would save or gain each year if you used this product.

Basically, they said that if you buy my product, it's free plus a profit. You pay up front to get the product in place, but after that it pays for itself, and then it goes on paying over and over again, year after year. So the more of our products you use, the more profitable you will be. You'll get rich paying money for our products; the more of our products you buy, the richer you'll become, and the faster.

This technique made IBM the world champion. They were rated as the best company in the world year after year by big business magazines, including *Fortune.*

Many people associated with IBM became rich. At one point, I think it was around 1962, IBM was making so many sales that they announced that salespeople could earn $100,000 commission; after that, they would be working on company time. They wouldn't earn any more.

One IBM salesman, named Ross Perot, said, "What about me?" He was such a great salesman that he hit $100,000 in commission income by January 24. So he went out and he started his own company. He became one of the richest people in America, but he used the same thing: the internal rate of return.

IBM had a very good marketing strategy. They would say, "Help me to understand how your business works and what you have to pay in order to process certain activities in your business—people, staff, taxes, machinery, equipment, and so on. Then let me come back to you with a proposal, and let us show you that we can make our product free to you. I'll be back in ten days. I will bring a proposal. You can have your top people here, your accountants. You can look at it and tell me what you think." No effort to sell at all. The most amazing darn thing.

Everybody would be eager to see this presentation. They would take it away, try it out, test it, and see if it was correct or not. Then they would come back. The only question was, "How soon can we pay hundreds of thousands of dollars for your product? How soon can we get it installed? How soon can we start using it?" There was no question about yes, no, maybe, discounts, or anything else. It was just how soon they could get the product.

I've used that strategy myself over the years, because especially in B2B—business to business—they are hoping or expecting to earn more money than the cost of the product. The product is supposed to generate greater savings on the downside or greater revenues on the upside. If it doesn't, the company shouldn't buy it, and you shouldn't be selling it.

Therefore you have to be crystal clear about how much better off your customer will be if they buy and use your product or service. You have to persuade them of that and prove it.

Recently a friend of mine took out a full-page ad in *USA Today* on marketing strategy. It said, "Hire me, and I will give you $120,000 of marketing strategy consulting free." It's a very gutsy proposal, but I know how he does it. He is offering what is called a *risk reversal*, which basically says, "There is always a risk in the purchase of any new product or service, so I will offer you my product or service, and I will structure it so that if you do not get the benefits that I say, there will be no charge. I'll reverse the risk, so that all of it is on me; you have no risk at all. If you are not successful, there's no charge. If you are successful, you're going to make or save an enormous amount of money."

To make your sales and marketing more productive, structure an offer with a risk reversal; so if your customer does not get the benefits you promise, there is no charge.

He has the ability to put in full-page ads in national publications because that is a very good offer, and the phone rings off the hook. People say, "Please, please, take me. Sell me your product. Call on me. Bring me your product"—because of the clarity.

My friend says, "Let me take a look at your business, how it works, and how much it costs. Then I will tell you if I can offer you this risk reversal in the course of our transaction. If I can't, I won't sell it to you, and you won't have to buy it."

Some of the richest people in the world have been those who have been able to demonstrate that the cost of their product or service is low compared to the benefits that you'll get back. It's always about clarity.

The customer is going to ask, "First of all, why should I buy this product? Second, why should I buy it from you? And third, why should I buy it now?" Your answers must be clear.

Every decision maker who buys a product or service, especially in a business, has four questions, even if they don't ask them aloud:

1. How much does it cost? How much money do I have to give you to get the benefits that you're offering?
2. What benefit do I get exactly, quantified in numbers?
3. How soon do I get this benefit?
4. How fast do I get the benefit?

It's how much in, how much out? How fast, how sure? Your job is, in the course of your conversation, to answer all those questions. If you don't, the customer will have no choice but to say, "Let me think it over. I'll call you back. Send me something in the mail. Don't call me; I'll call you."

But if you can be clear about your answers, you can sell all you want to all the people you want to sell to.

Four questions every decision maker asks about your product/service:
1. How much does it cost?
2. What benefit do I get exactly, quantified in numbers?
3. How soon do I get this benefit?
4. How fast do I get the benefit?

The Power of Goals

For years I've talked about the power of goal setting. In this context, let's talk about using goals to be more productive in your career.

Every study that I've ever seen in my life—and I've studied this subject like a fanatic—says that only 3 percent of adults have written goals and plans. The other 97 percent have hopes and wishes and maybe jots on paper, but they don't have written goals and plans.

If you look at people who have the most money in any society, they all have goals. If you look at poor people in any society, they don't have goals. It's yes or no, black or white, up or down. Very simple.

In my public seminars, I've spoken to more than 5 million people. In almost every one of these seminars, I say let's get back to basics and let's talk about goals. Every single week, people come back to me and say, "You changed my life. You made me rich. You taught me about goals."

"What was it that I helped you with so much?"

They always say, "It was the goals. I went to the best schools. I come from the best family, but I never had any money. Then, within a month after writing down my goals, my life transformed. It was unbelievable."

Seven Steps for Goal Setting

I have a remarkably effective seven-step process for goal setting, and I've taught it all over the world.

STEP 1: DECIDE WHAT YOU WANT

I've already talked about clarity. Step number one is always for you to *decide exactly what you want in any area of your life.* Your goal is what you want to end up with at the end of the day, what you want to accomplish. What is it that you want to be, have, or do?

You must also be specific. You must be so clear about your goal that you could explain it to a five-year-old child, and the child could turn to another person and tell them exactly what it is, and this third person would understand your goal.

STEP 2: WRITE IT DOWN

Step number two is *write it down.* It has to be written down; you can't type it. There's a reason for this. I've seen this study duplicated over and over through the years: University students who type out their notes on their laptops remember nothing of what they wrote down. Whereas people who write out their notes by hand—even if they have average intelligence and come from average backgrounds—run circles around the geniuses who type them out, because the geniuses forget everything they typed out by the time they close their laptop at the end of the class.

So you have to write it down. When you do, it's like writing it onto your superconscious mind. You're writing it onto a screen, if you like. When you stop writing, it automatically gets transferred to your superconscious mind.

You've heard about the law of attraction, which basically says that you attract into your life the people and circumstances that are in harmony with your dominant thoughts. So your most important goal is to become absolutely clear about those dominant thoughts. If you think failure thoughts, if you think worry thoughts, if you think money-losing thoughts, you're going to attract those things into your life.

Most people use this incredible power in opposition to themselves. They think about what they're worried about—

their bills and their problems and the people who may do them dirty. Surprise, surprise! They keep attracting negative people into their lives, and whom did they associate with most of the time? People who complain and grumble about problems in their lives.

What do they think about? They lie awake at night thinking about negative things, and they keep setting up this force field of energy. Remember, every person is like a hidden magnet. Every person has this magnet in their brain. Just as a magnet attracts iron particles, they attract into their lives people and circumstances that are in harmony with those pictures and ideas, especially if they're emotionalized.

Emotionalizing a goal—which is what you do when you write it down and reread it—is like electrifying the goal and giving it even more power and strength. So when you write down your goal in a positive way, you set up a force field of energy that starts to vibrate and starts to draw into your life people, circumstances, ideas, and insights that make your goals come true.

STEP 3: SET A DEADLINE

Number three is *set a deadline*. The deadline tells your subconscious mind, which then supplies your superconscious mind with the working materials about when you want the goal. Your superconscious mind has to know. You don't say, "I want to be rich sometime in the future," because that could mean thirty or forty years.

Again, it's about clarity. Many people that have been through my seminars have said to me, "I wasted years of my life simply by not being clear. How could this incredible supercon-

---

When you have clear goals and plans, you are forced to become organized because you have a clear destination toward which you are moving.

---

scious computer that I have in my brain work if I don't instruct it, if I don't give it any direction or guidance?"

I'll use an example. Imagine you call a nice restaurant, and you say, "Hello, my name is Brian Tracy. I'd like to come for dinner at your restaurant."

The person on the other end would ask, "When would you like to come?"

"Well, I'm not sure."

"How many people would be coming?"

"I haven't decided that yet."

"What time in the evening would you want to make this reservation for?"

"I haven't confirmed that either, but I would still like to make a reservation and have you honor it when I show up."

The person on the other end would probably conclude that you needed a checkup from the neck up, because you cannot even make a reservation for dinner if you don't know those simple facts.

Therefore, imagine your superconscious mind has this incredible power, and it can bring you anything you want in life, but you have to be clear about what it is.

I'll give you a quick example, which I don't share with many people. Many years ago, when I started working on goals, I was single, and I wanted to meet the ideal woman for me. I knew that goal setting worked, because I had used it. I said, if goal setting works for getting a car, getting a job, getting money, what about finding the perfect person?

So I wrote down a description of the perfect person for me. I wrote down maybe twenty-five things that I wanted in the perfect person, and surprise, surprise—in a matter of weeks, that perfect person walked into my life. I met her, I looked at her, she looked at me, we went out for coffee, we went out for dinner, and we began a relationship that lasted almost two years.

I had neglected some things in my description: calm, positive, cheerful, and a normal personality. She was a crazy person. Every single person has had a neurotic partner in their life that taught them a lot about what they want and what they don't want.

A couple of years later, I met my current wife, Barbara, who was single at the time. We were both taking courses at the local university. She was not sure about what to do with her life, and she said, "How would I find the ideal person for me?"

"It's quite simple," I said. "You just sit down, and you write out a list of everything that you want in the perfect person for you."

"How could that work?"

"Don't worry," I said. "It works."

"But isn't that kind of coldhearted or inflexible or unromantic?"

"No, it's not. It's unromantic to find yourself with the wrong person and have your life scrambled for an extended period of time."

"Interesting idea," she said.

We went our separate ways. I went home, and I thought it was about time I wrote a new list. So I sat down with a piece of paper, and I wrote out my list. I had about forty qualities I wanted in the perfect person for me, and they included *normal, levelheaded, friendly, compassionate, personable, easygoing, relaxed, open, flexible.*

Time passed, and one day I got a call from Barbara, who said, "I followed your advice, and I would like to share my results with you."

"OK," I said. "I'll meet you at the university."

I met her and I said, "What did you find out?"

"I wrote down everything that you said, and I decided exactly who is the perfect person for me."

"That's great. What did you come up with?"

She said, "It's you."

I was taken aback, but I thought it over, and I looked at my list. Later we realized that each of us had described the other person perfectly. We got married, and we've been married for forty years.

Does this work in business? I had a great new product that I had developed in my business, and I needed a super person to come and work for me, largely on commission, to sell this product into the market. So I wrote down a list of thirty-two things I wanted in the perfect person. Two days later, my phone rang. It was a very competent executive, who was between jobs and had heard of me in the past. He was wondering if he could come in and talk to me about working for my company. I don't normally take that kind of an invitation, but I did.

He came in, and I said, "I have about 30 minutes, and then I have to get going." I spent three hours with him, and I hired him, which I never do—I never hire a person on the first call. He came to work for me, and he did an outstanding job. He was brilliant, competent, capable, creative, a great salesman, a great marketer, everything.

About a month later, I sat him down and said, "I want to show you something. It's a system that I teach to other people, and I used it with you. It's a description of you before I met you." We sat down and went over the list, and he had every single item that I had written down, and six or seven more besides. He could do computer programming, he could do marketing plans online. He could interconnect with the data systems of other companies including potential customers for us. He was unbelievable.

So does it work? Yes, it works. The benefits that you will get from writing clear descriptions forces you to think clearly—just from writing it down.

When my wife and I got married, we ran out of money starting a business. We had to move to a rented house. We sat down and said, "OK, we don't want to live here forever, but where *do* we want to live?" We made a list. We wrote down forty-two things—we still have the list of the things that we wanted in our perfect house. We wrote them down, and bought magazines of beautiful homes, *Better Homes and Gardens, Architectural Digest*. We wrote those things down, and then went to work.

Two and a half years later, we moved into that house in a different state, in a different country, in a different city. It was the most remarkable thing, and we had to earn the money to be able to buy the house and pay for it.

So does it work? Yes, it works.

To sum up so far, step number one: decide exactly what you want so that you could explain it to a five-year-old. Step number two: write it down so that a five-year-old could read it and understand it clearly. Step number three: set a deadline. When do you want this goal to be achieved?

STEP 4: MAKE A LIST

Step number four is *make a list*. List making is one of the greatest skills for wealth and happiness ever discovered. A list forces you to think at the highest level and to activate your superconscious mind at the deepest level.

Write down every single thing that you could think of that you would possibly have to do to achieve that goal—everything you could think of. (This, by the way, often takes several runs at the paper.) You write it down, come back to it, write it down again, come back to it, and write it down. You may end up with two or three or four pages.

It's very much as if a company wanted to start a new business in a new market with a new product. They would sit down, and they would make a plan. They would write out a list of everything they were going to have to do to develop this new product.

You can imagine how many hundreds of pages of lists that Apple had when it brought out the first iPhone. They had something like 4,000 engineers working on the plans for the iPhone worldwide before they finally got to the point where they could announce it in San Francisco and bring it to the market.

STEP 5: ORGANIZE THE LIST

Step number five is *organize the list*. Organize the list by priority. There's a wonderful business book called *The Checklist Manifesto*. I've read it two or three times. For me, it's spellbinding. It talks about people who wrote out clear, detailed checklists in order—very complicated procedures—and accomplished them spotlessly and without a mistake. Others, with the greatest skill and knowledge and money, left out or deleted one key step. They ruined themselves and their businesses, and often they caused the deaths of many people.

The Checklist Manifesto says make a checklist. All success comes from making a checklist of everything that you will need to do to achieve the goal—in sequence, in order. What do you do first? What do you do second? What do you do third, and so on?

STEP 6: TAKE ACTION

Step number six is to *take action*. You have the checklist; you know what your goal is; you have your deadline. Take action. Move now. Get up. Stand up from where you are. Pick up the phone. Go onto the Internet, but do something immediately. Launch it. Kick it off, like a kickoff in a football game. Don't put it aside and say, "I have the goal, and it's written out."

You'll be astonished at what will happen if you just do that, because your superconscious mind is now working twenty-four hours a day to bring that goal into your life. In taking action, you trigger your mental powers, and you activate your super-conscious mind.

STEP 7: DO SOMETHING EVERY DAY

Step number seven is *do something every single day that moves you at least one step closer to your goal*. This is seven days a week, every single day. You can do more than one step if you like. You can work on the previous step much longer, but do one thing every day, seven days a week, until you achieve the goal.

If you do this, in many cases you will be your own worst enemy. You will be your own biggest critic. You'll probably set a goal that is ridiculous. "I want to become a millionaire." I remember setting that goal for myself many years ago, when I was living in a little rented apartment with rented furniture. I had almost no money at all, and I was selling and living on straight commission. I wrote down that I wanted to be a millionaire. I said, "What would be the steps I would have to take to become a millionaire?"

Knowing what I now know in terms of success psychology, this is what I would say.

1. Get up early every morning. All successful people get up early in the morning.

2. Write and rewrite your goals in the present tense. Take a piece of paper—I prefer a spiral notebook—and write down ten goals. You could write more than that, but your mind can only work comfortably on about ten to fifteen goals at a time. After that, it goes into overwhelm.

   Write these goals down in the present tense, as though you have already achieved them. Rather than writing, "I will achieve this goal," write, "I am a self-made millionaire by this particular date," and so on.

3. Read for one hour or more every day. Read something that is educational, that is spiritual, that is motivational. Read something that is protein for the mind, something that makes you feel better about yourself and your life.

4. Make a list and set priorities on the list.

5. Start work on your first priority, the most important thing that you can do, and work on it until it's complete.

6. Listen to audio programs in your car. Take every single minute of travel time and turn it into learning time. I

started off doing this when I was driving a car with a cassette player. Later I drove a car with a CD player. Today you can carry all your audio programs on your iPad, and you can take them with you when you exercise.

7. Ask yourself two questions after every experience. I call these the magic questions, and they will make you rich: (1) What did I do right in that last call or activity? (2) What would I do differently next time?

In short: What did I do right? What would I do differently? These are magic questions, because they force you to think positively about the best things that you did and the best things that you'll do in the future.

Two magic questions that will make you rich:
1) "What did I do right in that last call or activity?"
and 2) "What would I do differently next time?"

The 7 Steps for Productive Goal-Setting:

1. Decide what you want
2. Write It Down
3. Set a Deadline
4. Make a List—of every single thing that would help you to achieve your goal
5. Organize the list
6. Take Action
7. Do something every day—that moves you one step closer to your goal.

Those seven steps were great. I went to work on them, and I did them every single day. For seven months I didn't notice any difference. Then my income started to tick up. I did the steps for a year, and my income went higher. I continued to do them, and within five years my income increased ten times. So I kept doing those steps every day. Five years later, my income increased ten times more. It increased a total of 100 times in ten years.

I've given this advice to other people all over the world in every economic condition, and they've said that my projection was too conservative. They became millionaires, or they increased their income ten times in six or seven or eight years.

In any case, the last step in goal setting is to do something every day. This takes us back to self-discipline. Many times I've had people who have come to me saying, "I was bankrupt, I was an alcoholic, and I was divorced, and I began to follow your goal setting system. Today I'm rich. Today I have three businesses. I have a staff of thirty-eight. I've never had so much money in my life. You've changed my life. You've made me rich."

Now what is the downside on what I have just explained? There is none. There's zero downside. I'm not asking you to go out and pay a fortune for a success system that may or may not work. I'm asking you to invest a little bit of your time in your future with the knowledge that I've used with hundreds of thousands of people in eighty-three countries, not one of whom has ever said it didn't work. I've never had a letter, an email, or a personal contact that said, "I followed your advice, and it didn't work." But 100 percent of the people who have said that they followed my advice say it worked like a dream. "I accomplished more and faster than I ever dreamed possible."

One guy took me to the airport in his new Mercedes-Benz. He'd just started with his new sales job a year before when he came to my course. Other people have beautiful new homes, houses in the mountains, and they take ski trips at ski resorts. They go to beautiful restaurants, and they're having wonderful lives.

The people who appreciate this the most are working people, who came from average families, went to average schools, and came from average neighborhoods, and today they're rich. Everybody looks up to them, and their families admire them for what they've accomplished. They wink and nod, and say, "It was so simple. It's guaranteed to work."

That is my advice to you with regard to setting and achieving goals: write them down, work on them every day, and you will be astonished at what happens. In forty years of teaching this concept, I've never had a failure story.

I knew a man who was taking courses at the university. He took a course in chemistry and fell in love with it. He set a goal and wrote it down. He said, "I am going to become so good at chemical science that I get a Nobel Prize."

He was twenty-two when he made that goal for himself, and he was forty-two when he walked up onto the stage and received the Nobel Prize for chemical theory. He received it in conjunction with two other world-class scientists.

"I never doubted," he told me. "I always knew I would receive a Nobel Prize. I watched the Nobel Prizes on television. I read about the Nobel Prize recipients. On vacation one year, I went to Stockholm, where they give out the Nobel Prizes. I just immersed my mind, and I worked and worked.

"Then one day I came up with a breakthrough, and I found that there were two other scientists, one in the U.S. and one in Europe, who were also working in this area. I communicated with them, and we met. We pooled our ideas, and together we won a Nobel Prize.

"With that prize, I'm now a tenured professor at one of the best universities in the world. My income is higher than anything I ever dreamed I would ever earn, and I'm surrounded by the best and smartest people in the world. I'm working with the students from the best homes in the country. I worked on my goal for twenty years, and I never doubted."

This is what happens when you have clear goals and plans. You are forced to become organized. If you don't have goals, it's like driving a car with no steering wheel in a huge parking lot. It just goes here and goes there. Your life goes back and forth; you stop, you quit, and anybody can interrupt you (especially with online activities). Anything can stop you from working, because you have no goal. You have no direction. You have no destination.

But once you have that destination, you keep saying, "Back to work. Back to work." You do only those things that move you toward the completion of your most important task each day.

Faith and trust are key to this whole process. Imagine that somebody who has great powers, who's never wrong and never fails, could guarantee that you would achieve a particular goal, and just proceed every day as though the goal is absolutely slam-dunk guaranteed.

One of my favorite stories is about a top businessman. The son of a friend of his got into sales. He got an appointment with this businessman, and he came to see him. The young man said, "I've finished college, and I'm getting into sales now. My father arranged this appointment. I wonder if you could help me find some prospects for my product."

"I'm glad you asked me," he said, "but why would you come to me?"

"Because you know so many people. You must have some names."

"Yes," he said, "I know a lot of people. Let me get you a list." He went out, went to his secretary, and the secretary came back with a list all typed up, with names, addresses, phone numbers.

"Here's a list of ten people who are very good prospects," said the businessman. "You could call on them."

The young man went out, and he called on those people, and he was really enthusiastic. He was really happy—he was starting off his career with referrals from one of the most important businesspeople in the city. He made five sales out of the ten. He came back the following week.

"I wanted to thank you so much," said the young man. "You've launched my career. I'm ahead of anybody else I started with. Is there any way I could get another list of names?"

"Absolutely. Just a minute."

The businessman went out of the room, and he came back with the city telephone directory. "Here you go," he said. "Here's the Yellow Pages, with all the companies in this field. There are several hundred. This is where I got the first ten names, and now you can pick your own ten."

The young man was shocked. He had been so confident that he was going to make a sale because he had been given the names of what he thought were personal friends of this powerful businessman.

There's a famous story of a baseball coach whose team was in a slump. They had lost several games. The coach came to the team and said, "I've heard that there is a magic man in this city, a person who can cast spells. Maybe he can help us break out of this slump. I want you all to give me your favorite bat, and I'm going to take it to him and ask him if he would bless these bats."

They said, "OK." They were all in a slump. They were all depressed.

The coach took ten or fifteen bats, and he went off for the afternoon. He came back at the end of the day, and he handed out the bats. He said, "This magic guy placed a spell on these bats. He said these are going to be home-run bats all day tomorrow."

The next day these guys went out there, and they smacked home run after home run. They couldn't believe the number of home runs this team made. The team was absolutely delighted. They were so happy, and then they said, "Great. We can take these bats, and we're going to win the league."

One of the others said, "I wasn't here yesterday, and I didn't get my bat blessed. Is it possible that I could do that today?"

"I have to tell you the truth," said the coach. "There was no magic man. I just took the bats, put them in my car for the day, and brought them back. The magic was in your mind. The magic was in your confidence that you would bat home runs the following day."

Remember, it's all between your ears. It's how much confidence you have. The most wonderful affirmation, which sounds so simple, is, "I can do it. I can do it. I like myself, and I can do it."

When I was in sales, I created my own affirmation, and I have shared it with a million salespeople. It is, "I like myself, and I love my work." No matter what field that you are in today, when you get up in the morning, say to yourself, "I love my work. I love myself, and I love my work. I love my work. I love my work."

If you can't say it for any period of time, that will tell you something. It may mean that you're in the wrong job. Now please understand this: It doesn't mean that the job is wrong. It doesn't mean that the company is bad. It doesn't even mean that your boss or your product or anything else is bad or wrong. It just means that it's not right for you.

In dating, they say you have to kiss a lot of horny toads before you meet the handsome prince. When you date, you meet many different members of the opposite sex. You'll get along with some of them for a short time, and some not at all. But if a relationship doesn't work out, it's not because there's something wrong with the other person. It's just that you weren't suited; that's all.

It's amazing how many people are unhappy for years because they had a relationship that didn't work out. It's not personal. Some relationships work out, some don't. If you have a job, and you don't like the job, or the company, it doesn't mean it's a bad company. You never have to badmouth the company or the person, because this kind of thing just happens. One of the most powerful lines is, *it just happens*. The chemistry wasn't there.

The Best Time Management System

Years ago, people had time management organizing systems they would carry with them—Day-Timers, for example. Today there is a new generation of digital apps and tools to make people more effective and stay on track with their commitments.

Here's my experience with these systems. Years ago, I was asked to produce an audio program on time management. I began to read different books and articles about the subject. I found that there were four major companies in the U.S. that gave one-day time management seminars; these were combined with time management planners. They taught you how to organize your time, set your goals, get more done, plan each day, and so on.

I traveled to all four cities where I could learn these systems. One was in Toronto, another was in New York, another in Denver, another in Los Angeles. I traveled, spent a full day on each seminar, took notes, and wrote down everything. I sent away for the time management systems from all over the country, as well as one from Denmark. A good friend of mine is Danish, and he ordered it and translated it for me. It was the most popular one in Europe at that time.

I set them all down and worked them all out. I put together a time management system of my own. When the computers came out, I bought each time planner that I could find and worked with it. I found that I could not discipline myself to keep with any one of these systems.

Then *Inc.*, the business magazine, did a study. They interviewed fifty entrepreneurs, presidents of fast-growing companies, and they asked them what their favorite time management system was. Every single one of them picked a blank yellow page. They said their favorite time management system was a pad of paper on which they wrote down everything they had to do in the course of the day. They organized that list by priority—by which thing needs to be done first. "If I could only do one thing today before I was called out of town for a month, which one job would I want to be sure to get completed? Then I would start with number one and work on that. That was the primary reason for my becoming the president of a very successful company." The best time management system still seems to be a piece of paper and a pen.

Expensive and complex time management and productivity systems are unnecessary. The best time management system is a piece of paper and a pen.

The rule is that you will save ten minutes in execution for every minute you spend in planning. It takes about ten to twelve minutes for you to make out a list and organize it at the beginning of the day. It's even better to do it the night before, so that when you go to sleep, your subconscious mind works on that list all night long. Sometimes when you wake up in the morning, you'll have breakthrough ideas that will change your life and make you rich.

You make out your organized list the night before, and you set priorities. The next morning, start with the number one goal that you've already decided on. Making out the list will take about twelve minutes and will save you about two hours. If you take that two hours, and you use it on your most valuable tasks, you will become more and more productive, higher and higher paid. You'll get more and more opportunities. Your mind will get sharper and sharper, and not only you will achieve your goals, but you'll become rich.

"You will save ten minutes in preparation for every minute you spend in planning." —Brian Tracy

---

An Action Step

Let me wrap up this chapter with an action step. Some years ago, I offered an entrepreneurial coaching program in which I would bring thirty or forty entrepreneurs to San Diego and work with them for a complete day four times a year. My guarantee was that if you followed the exercises, which were structured to go day by day, and if you applied the plan that you organized during your day with me, you would double your income and double your time off. If you didn't—here's risk reversal at work—there would be no charge for the program; I would refund 100 percent of what you paid to attend.

I gave the program for seven years. I put about four or five groups of entrepreneurs through the program every year. At the end of seven years, I was so busy with other things that I brought it to an end, but I never had a single request for a refund.

People doubled and tripled their incomes in as little as seven days. Some people doubled their income the next week, even before seven days were up. Everybody doubled their income. Some of them doubled and tripled their income and spent more time with their family than they'd ever done before.

At the beginning of the first sessions, I would hand out a spiral notebook, like a school notebook, to each one of my students. I would say, "I want to introduce you today to your new best friend. I'm giving this to you because I don't want to have to give any refunds. I can guarantee that if you will use this spiral notebook, you will not be able to claim a refund, because you will more than double your income and double your time off."

In the course of the morning, I would teach them to take out this notebook and write down ten goals that they would like to accomplish in the next twelve months.

That's what I would like you to do now. Get a notebook, and write down ten goals that you'd like to achieve. Write them in the present tense. "I earn this amount of money by December 31 of this year. I weigh this number of pounds by this particular date in this year. I make this trip or release this product, start this business—" whatever your goals are. You can have business goals, financial goals, health goals, and of course, family goals.

Write down the ten goals, and write them in the present tense, as though you have already accomplished them. Your subconscious mind cannot focus on a goal that is not written in the present tense, so write it in the present tense, as though it already exists, and you're explaining to someone else: "I earn $1 million a year. I earned twice as much this year as I earned last year. I earned ten times the amount that I was earning five years ago" or whatever it happens to be.

Keep your goals within twelve months. These goals are far more motivational, far more powerful, than anything else. Then each morning, when you start off, ask, "If I could only complete one task today, which one task would it be? If I needed to complete one task before I was called out of town for a month, which would it be?"

Then review your list of planned activities for the day. Put a circle around the one you choose. Step number three is begin work on that task, and work on it single-mindedly, as if the house were on fire and you had to complete the task before the flames got to you.

Write it down. Work and work nonstop on that one most important task until it's complete, and don't do anything else. Don't talk to your friends. If someone says, "Hey, do you have a moment to talk?" you say, "Yes, but it'll have to be after work. Right now, I have to get this job done. I have to get this job done. I have to get it done today. I am behind."

Nobody will bother you. As soon as you tell them you have to get a job done, they'll back off. If they come again, tell them again, "I'm not done yet. I have to get this job done." Pretty soon, as I said before, they'll stop bothering you.

Do these three things: (1) each morning, write down your ten goals in the spiral notebook in the present tense, (2) plan your day and select task number one, and then (3) go to work on it immediately.

I remember when I began teaching this process. A gentlemen came to my program, and he said he had been going to another coaching program. He had paid $25,000 a year for it, and he'd gone for three years. He said accomplished more with this list of ten goals within one month than he'd accomplished in three years at a cost of $75,000. He could not believe it. His life, his business, everything, transformed almost overnight.

So does it work? Yes. There has never been a person who has said it didn't work, so the only question is, will *you* work? Will you do it? Do you have the discipline to start, the discipline to continue, and the discipline to finish?

What To Do Now!:

1. Get a spiral notebook or a pad of paper, and write down ten goals you would like to achieve, and write them in the present tense, as if you had already accomplished them. For example, "I earn X amount of money by December 31st of this year."
2. Plan your day and select task #1
3. Go to work on it immediately.

Chapter Four

Breakthrough Habits
to Get Organized Now!

Organization is a matter of habit, and all habits are learned and learnable. Telling yourself that you are not an organized person is merely a cop-out. It's not true.

Being disorganized means that you must always work for people who *are* organized. If you're not organized or working towards your goal step-by-step, you must always work for someone else who can discipline you and keep on your case.

Very few people are disorganized geniuses, although there are a couple out there. Many people hold onto stories about people like Richard Branson, who has 200 businesses but who is

---

**Choosing to be disorganized means that you
must always work for people who *are* organized.
Fortunately, organization is not an inherent
personality trait—it is a learned skill.**

---

dyslexic. They'll say he's not organized. Maybe he can't read or construct sentences, but look at how Richard Branson runs his life. He knows what his weaknesses are. He's not an organized person, but he has a good sense of what would make a good business, and he knows people, markets, and competition. He explores a new business opportunity until he has a good sense of it. Then he starts to ask around to see who's the best person in this field. He finds that this best person is probably a senior executive at another company—maybe an identical company to what he's thinking about starting, like Virgin Air or Virgin Records. He'll go to them and say, "I'm thinking of starting a company in this area. Would you be interested in working with me to help me to do it?"

The person would say, "What's in it for me?"

"If you help me build this company, I'll share its success with you. I'll provide the financial resources to get started, and you'll provide the experience and brainpower to make it work. How does that sound?"

The person says, "That's great."

The organizing is meticulous, but it's not done by Richard. He recognizes that's not his strong suit. He hires someone else to do the organizing. His skill is finding organizers rather than organizing.

If you're not a Richard Branson, you need to be organized. Wonderfully, organization is a learnable skill, and you can learn it and become excellent at it if you want to do it badly enough.

Now here's my proof. If you join the military, the first thing they do is teach you how to march, dress, drill, and get out of bed in the morning. There's a famous book that's called *Make*

Your Bed. It goes onto the best-seller list at graduation time every year at the major universities.

A successful general gave a commencement talk called "Make Your Bed." He said that in the military, especially in the officers' corps, when you get out of bed, you stand up, and you immediately turn to your bed. You make it up so tight that you can drop a coin on the bed, and it will bounce. That's how tight the cover is.

Then you turn and dress. You shower, shave, dress meticulously, put on your tie, and polish your shoes so that you look first-class when you begin your day. You do this every day. They have you do this routine probably for your first six months in officer training. You get up, make the bed, drop a coin on the bed, and have it bounce.

As the general explained in his address, if you complete a task first thing each morning, you will be shifted into task completion mode for the rest of the day. You will be tuned on; you'll be revved up. If you develop the habit of completing a task first thing in the morning, you'll be completing tasks all day long.

Remember, task completion is the key to success in life, and if you just complete a small task, it gives you a jolt of endorphins, which are called nature's happy drug. They give you a buzz, and you feel happy. You feel elated. Your self-esteem and self-confidence go up, and you feel like a winner.

If you complete a task first thing in the morning, your self-esteem and self-confidence will go up and you will be shifted into task completion mode for the rest of the day.

As I said, when I wake up, I get up and immediately do physical exercise. That gets you pumped up. It gets your heart rate up. It gets your brain engorged with highly-oxygenated blood, which makes you smarter all day long, and when you get your brain engorged with blood, it again, releases endorphins. You want to do more stuff.

Start off with your most important task, begin on that task, and work on it until it's completed. At night, write down the tasks that you're going to do tomorrow. There is a saying that *positive prior planning prevents poor performance.* Get together everything that you are going to need to complete the task, and have it all sitting there ready to go before you begin. Assembling the necessary materials is a real motivator. Then begin and discipline yourself to stay at it until it's complete. Do this every single day with every single task.

As I said earlier, you must have a list of steps that you need to take. I mentioned *The Checklist Manifesto.* You need a checklist for a task—how you're going to do it. It's very much like a recipe. If you're going to make a dish, take a recipe, follow it exactly the way the chef has written it, and you will make the dish about 80 percent as well as a professional chef.

My favorite salad is a Caesar salad. I used to go to restaurants that served great Caesar salad at the tableside. They'd bring out all the ingredients and a big bowl, and the waiter standing next to the table would mix up the salad and serve it. It was always great.

One day I said to myself, "This guy is not a genius. He's just a waiter, yet he makes a beautiful Caesar salad every time we come here. I'm going to learn how to do it myself." That sent me into a long process in which I got cookbooks and bor-

---

The message of *The Checklist Manifesto*, is that you must have a checklist for every task, and the exact steps that you will follow to complete the task—just like a recipe.

---

rowed recipes from my mother. I bought a salad bowl and all the ingredients, and I practiced and practiced. Now I make one of the best Caesar salads in the world. My Caesar salad, Brian Tracy's Caesar Salad, is on my website, briantracy.com, and it's free. People who use it to make a Caesar salad just blow away everybody in the house; they say it's the best Caesar salad they're ever had. But at one time, I could not make the salad at all. At one time, I could barely track the ingredients aside from saying this is romaine lettuce, and these are croutons. Now I can make a Caesar salad.

Any skill that you want to develop, you can learn simply by practice, by becoming absolutely clear that you want to be very good at it.

Many years ago, I got an offer from a major publisher to write a book, but I could not type. I could only do the hunt-and-peck method. This method enables you to type five to eight words per minute, and five to eight words a minute to write 60,000 words (about the normal length for a nonfiction book) would take me weeks or months, so I said, "I'm going to have to learn how to type."

So I bought a loadable program with a series of lessons that are each about ten or fifteen minutes long. It's called *Mavis Beacon Teaches Typing*. I've mentioned it to people over the years, and they all say, "Oh, we love Mavis," because it took them from hunt-and-peck typing to being able to type fluently.

Within ninety days, you can type sixty to eighty words a minute. You can touch-type, and you'll never look at a keyboard again.

As of this year, I have written eighty-seven books, and I have three or four planned out. I have publishers, including the biggest publisher in the world, ready for them, because they're so happy with the previous ones. But at one time I could not type a page.

You can learn anything you need to learn. Some people will have a natural ability for certain skills, and other people will take much longer, but anyone can do it.

Many years ago, I got a job working for the big boss I mentioned earlier. Through a series of coincidences, he had seen me at work; I had done some real estate development. He offered me a job as his personal assistant at his $850 million company. At the time I was single, in my early thirties, and not going very far in life. I accepted it. I was so happy.

He worked me hard. He really wanted to get a lot of work out of me. He didn't talk very much, but he gave me lots of work to do. I did everything quickly and well. It changed my life forever. I was never the same, because I had the opportunity to do things quickly and well and developed a reputation for getting organized. He was watching me, and other people were watching me. He was watching me because he wanted me to be successful; the other senior executives were watching me because they *didn't* want me to be successful.

Getting organized is challenging to start with, but then it becomes automatic and easy. It's like driving a car or riding a bicycle or typing on a keyboard. Once you have it, you have it for life.

Eat That Frog

Some years ago the owner of a major publishing house asked me if I would write a book for them. I sent a book I'd written to him; it was called *Double Your Income and Double Your Time Off.* He got back to me the following week, and he said, "It's a great concept because everybody wants to have the benefit that you're offering, but it's not really very appealing. It's not sexy. However, in the book you talk about Mark Twain."

Mark Twain was famous for writing "The Celebrated Jumping Frog of Calaveras County," and he used frogs as a metaphor. He said that if the first thing you do when you get up in the morning is eat a live frog, you'll have the pleasure of knowing it's probably the worst thing that's going to happen to you all day. I'd read the story when I was young.

"There are two corollaries to this rule," said the publisher. "One is, if you have two frogs to eat, eat the ugliest one first. Corollary number two is, if you have to eat a frog at all, it doesn't pay to sit and look at it for very long." In other words, get on with it.

That was in chapter 15 of my book. "I really like this chapter," said the publisher. "If you could take this chapter and make it the title of the book, and then run all the other chapters on time management throughout that book, and make eating the frog your most valuable and most important task, I think we would have an interesting approach. Right now, there are two or three books with animals in the titles. There's *Who Moved My Cheese?* There's *Fish.* Maybe this will work."

So I wrote it up, and I sent it back to them. They said, "Bingo. This works," and they published it. It's called *Eat that*

**Always tackle the ugliest (toughest/longest) task first
and don't look at it and stew over it for very long.**

---

*Frog: 21 Great Ways to Stop Procrastinating and Get More Things
Done Faster.* It contains the twenty-one best ideas in time management ever discovered, and every one of them is about two or
three pages long. There's about 110 pages.

We released the book, and it took off. It became a *New York
Times* best seller. It went into many foreign languages. It sold
and sold, millions of copies now. It's been the best-selling book
for as many as two or three years in many countries around the
world.

I'm not telling you to buy that book. I'm just saying that it
organizes the process of getting organized. Countless people
have bought a thousand copies for their companies, and they've
created programs to teach these principles to their staff. They
have transformed their companies. People become wealthy
through the simple principle of picking their most important
task, getting started on it, and completing it. It's so simple; people do it, and pretty soon it becomes a habit. Every morning
they make their bed, if you like. They start off and complete
their most important task until it becomes a habit, and they can
hardly wait to start.

Here's something else that will help in terms of getting
organized. I always work from a list. Some of the tasks are
long—they take two or three hours—while some are shorter. If
my wife comes into my office at ten minutes to 7:00 and says it's
time for dinner, I have ten minutes to complete a task. I'll go
over my list and find a ten-minute task. I put my head down,

go full blast, and finish that task in nine or ten minutes. Then I shut off my lights and shut down my office. I walk out, and I feel great for the rest of the evening.

At one time Henry Ford was bankrupt and working out of his garage, but he became incredibly wealthy. He said any task can be completed if you break it down into enough small tasks. Break it down into small bits, and just do one. That gives you confidence. It raises your self-esteem. It gives you energy. It makes you happy, and it motivates you, like two hands shoving you from behind into the next step.

Plan Everything

One key idea for personal organization is plan everything in advance. Explain exactly what you mean by this idea. Is this practical? Is it true that everything in life can be planned in advance, or does this rule only apply to important goals?

If it's stopping to get a cup of coffee at Starbucks, there's not a lot to planning in advance, but there is a little. You're going to have to find a parking space. You're going to have to go in and get in line. You're going to have to decide where you're going to drink it in the café or take it home. Maybe you'll get a cup of coffee for someone else. (By the way, everybody's gotten into trouble by getting a cup of coffee from Starbucks and going back to the office. Someone else will say, "Why didn't you get me a cup? You know I drink coffee.")

Some planning is involved even with little things like that. Ask, and be sure that you're covering all your bases.

Of course planning is most important for tasks that are going to make the most difference in your life. The wonderful thing is that the more time you take to think the plan through, the more confidence you will have when you begin. The more rested you'll feel, the more focused, and so on.

Always take the time to plan. When great generals plan campaigns, they bring in their other generals and senior officers. They all get together, and they go through the plan over and over. Everybody is asked to contribute. As a result, when they launch the plan, it's amazing.

Once I worked with Norman Schwarzkopf, the general in charge of the Gulf War. He had 300,000 people under his command from twenty-two countries. I had studied his work. I knew what he had done and the successes he'd had.

Schwarzkopf said that they spent six months planning Operation Desert Storm, which was the campaign that destroyed the Iraqi Army. It took six months of planning out the intricacies, and then they launched the attack. It took 104 hours to destroy the third-biggest army in the world. The Iraqi army was absolutely destroyed, and the war was over. It was the greatest single victory in the shortest period of time, with the lowest number of casualties, ever achieved. He said it was all because of planning.

The Questionnaire

How much planning should you put into an activity? As a professional speaker—and I've given more than 5,000 talks in eighty-three countries over the years—I almost always arrange to do the talk with a conference call. It's basically an audition. "We're going to pay you a lot of money to come in and speak to a lot of people," they say. "We want to be sure that we're making the right decision, so let's go through some questions."

Many years ago I wrote a questionnaire, which I ask them to complete so I can have it in front of me when we talk. It asks a whole series of questions that clarify what the talk is going to be about and what they want it to accomplish.

Then I go onto their website and get their brochures and financial statements. I collect this material and study it in detail, so by the time I pick up the phone, I'm very knowledgeable about the company, how long it's been in business, what its major products and services are, and how well it's doing.

One time, I had an opportunity to speak for several days for an organization that had 40,000 employees and a budget of $50 billion. I was given all of the background information for the last year in the company, and it turned into sixteen hours of preparation to give my basic talk to get the job.

I got all the research, and I said, "Oh, my God!" I began on Saturday morning at about 8:00. I began writing, reviewing, and taking notes. I ended up with piles and pages of stuff.

So when I stood up to offer myself for this job in front of their board of directors, they said, "Oh, my God! You really know our business, don't you? You really understand how our business works, the key people, the products, the market we're dealing with." The president of organization said, "It's done. You're hired," and sat back down.

It also depends upon how much basic information you already have. When I first went to work with companies in certain industries, I would have to do a lot of research so that I really understood the industry. Now I can do ten or fifteen minutes' worth, which just builds on my previous research, because I really know the business. They hire me because they know that I really know their industry.

Ask the question how much you would invest, if you were in danger of losing this opportunity. If it's really important, take your time. Pay the price in advance.

Planning and Organization

- A key idea for personal organization is to *plan everything in advance*. Everything—from small tasks to large, life-changing tasks.
- Always take time to plan. How much time depends on the level of previous knowledge and experience you have completing a given task. To help determine how much time, ask yourself: How much time would I invest, if I were in danger of losing this opportunity?

Neatness Counts

Neatness is also key. When your workspace is neat and everything is put away, and you have only the things that you need to prepare for your job, you're going to do a much better job, make far fewer mistakes, and take less time.

So the first thing you do is prepare. You clear out your space. You put away everything that is not necessary. Even if you have to take everything on your desk and put it on the floor behind you, get it off your desk so that your mind and your eyes are uncluttered. You're looking straight at a clean desk, and you're working only on one thing.

It's amazing to me how many people want to write a book, but they never get on with it, because they never get organized.

They never lay it all out. Their working environment is cluttered. A cluttered working environment tires your mind. It distracts you and makes you fatigued. You're picking things up and putting them down. Suddenly you're out of time, and you haven't produced anything.

It's like making your bed. Your first discipline is to clean your work environment so everything is laid out, and you have just what you need to work with in front of you. Then begin.

One great technique you can use is to stand back and look at your working environment. Look at your desk. Look at where you work. Look at your briefcase, and say, "What kind of a person works at a desk like that?" Say you've been really busy, you've been working on a lot of different things, and your desk looks like a grenade just went off on it. What kind of a person would work at a desk like that?

I was reading the memoirs of a very successful entrepreneur, who built several million-dollar fortunes for himself and others. They had a clean-desk philosophy at work. They said, "Every day you finish your work by cleaning your desk completely, so there's not even a pen on the desk. You start every morning with a spotless desk." He said it was one of the most important business principles, because it forced people to put things away as they moved along. Nobody wanted to be there at 6:00 still putting away clutter, so they put things away, and they moved along.

Start and complete a task, and put it away. When you get into the rhythm of doing that, soon it becomes automatic and easy.

Imagine that somebody with responsibility in your company comes by, and your office looks as if it just had an explosion on it. I had a gentleman working for me some years ago whom I let go, and for good reason. His desk always looked as if he had dumped a wastebasket full of trash all over it.

If you are not well organized, you spend half of your time just looking for things, and you can't find them. Then three-quarters of the way through, you forget what you were looking for in the first place.

Keep moving forward, keep cleaning up, keep putting things away, and don't make any excuses.

No Excuses

We are all plagued with the excuse-making gland—excusitis. Instead of accepting responsibility, we say, "I could have done that, but I got caught up; I was talking to someone. I'll do it tomorrow."

It's quite astonishing how many of us use excuses to procrastinate ourselves into mediocrity and failure. We become poor. My book *No Excuses* is one of the best-selling books in the world. You know who loves it the most? The most disciplined and successful people in my seminars and workshops. They're the ones who need it the least, because they're so well organized, but they love the idea of discipline, organization, and personal constraints.

I believe that your willingness to accept responsibility for your work, your workplace, and your task completion is really the mark of the superior person. Superior people accept responsibility. Average people, inferior people, make excuses. They spend all their time thinking about how they're going to explain it away rather than spending the same amount of time getting the job done.

**Keep your desk clean and free of distractions.
Put away everything that is not necessary.
And only have materials on your desk that
pertain only to the immediate task at hand.**

Everyone has great intentions, but we know that the road to hell is paved with these. People say, "I'm going to do this and that. I'm going to start earlier, I'm going to work harder, and I'm going to save my money." Then they say, "Before I do anything, I need to take a little vacation to a wonderful place called Someday Isle. Someday I'll start saving, and someday I'll cut back on my expenses. Someday I'll do this, and someday I'll do that."

Whom are they surrounded with? Birds of a feather flock together, so they find themselves surrounded by other people on Someday Isle. They sit around and talk about their favorite excuses. "What's your excuse? What's your reason for being on the island this year?"

"I'm really tired, I didn't finish that last course, and the competition is really tough." They always have a reason for being on the island. But the key to success in life is to decide exactly what you want, write it down, and vote yourself off the island.

Preparation: The Mark of the Professional

Preparation is the mark of the professional. Preparation is absolutely key. I teach a special three-day program on how to speak professionally. If you come and spend three days with me in front of the video camera, and with eleven other people, I will show you how to get a standing ovation when you speak, even if you haven't spoken before.

I'm happily astonished at the number of people who write back to me after a few days or a few weeks, and they say they got this opportunity to speak. This always happens. There's a philosophical principle that I learned years ago: when you learn something new, you almost always get a chance to apply that new knowledge. It doesn't just disappear like cigarette smoke.

Let's say you take a first aid course, and you learn how to do the Heimlich maneuver. You're out at a restaurant, and a person starts to choke at the next table. You immediately jump up. You realize that they've eaten something and it's stuck in their throat. You do the Heimlich maneuver on them, and you save their life. You always get a chance to use the new information.

I was in a restaurant with my wife a few years ago, and we were having dinner. About two tables over, a man started grabbing his chest and choking, and he fell on the floor. Everybody said, "Oh, my God, he's choking." The people at his table were terrified. Everybody was paralyzed, like deer in the headlights.

"Excuse me, Barbara," I said. I got up and went over. I turned him over, and I pumped him and popped the steak out of his throat and got him breathing again. During this time, they had pulled back all the other tables and chairs, and everybody was watching this person and me working on him in the middle of the restaurant. He started breathing again, and he got up.

Meanwhile they had called an ambulance. The ambulance drivers came rushing in; they loaded him up on the gurney and took him out. Everything was fine. They brought all the tables and chairs back, and people resumed their dinners. I went back to the table and continued my conversation with Barbara.

When we walked out of the restaurant, the ambulance was still there, and the medics were still working on the guy. They said, "Whoever did that maneuver on him saved his life."

About two or three weeks later, we went back to the restaurant. When we were settling in, they brought us a bottle of champagne. They said, "It's a gift from us to you."

"What's it for?"

"Three weeks ago, you were in here, and that guy was choking." I didn't even remember; I had forgotten. "You saved his life."

"I did?" I said.

"Yeah, if you hadn't done that, the ambulance drivers told us that he would have been dead probably in another minute."

I had forgotten it completely until they brought me that bottle of champagne. My point is you'll never learn something new and helpful and not get an opportunity to use it.

In my program on how to become an excellent speaker, I teach the importance of preparation. One of my students was working with an engineering company. He was concerned because the other engineers were getting promoted faster and paid more, whereas he was doing busy work. They explained, "You have to understand. These people make presentations to our clients, and bring in business; they're called rainmakers." In a professional services firm, the rainmakers are the highest-paid and most respected people. They're the ones who get promoted more and paid more.

So this man took the course. About two or three days later, his boss came and said, "Look, we have a bit of a challenge. We have an important presentation to make, and I can't do it.

The engineer who was going to do it is out of town and can't get back. Could you do it for us?"

At first he was really nervous, and he said, "I don't know." Then he remembered what he had learned in this course. He said, "Yeah, I can do that; 90 percent is preparation. I can do the preparation, so give me all the information." He went out the next morning and gave a presentation on the company's services.

By the time the guy got back to the office, the president of the other company had phoned his boss. "That presentation was incredible. We want to hire you for this major project." It involved hundreds of thousands of dollars of revenues for the company. From then on, they sent him out every single time they had a client.

He jumped ahead several years in his career. Within another couple of years, he was a partner; his income went up 400 percent. He moved to a bigger house. He had a brand-new car. He had a great life. He had his own office and secretary. Everything happened because he had learned the skill of preparation so that when you stand up to speak, you are completely confident. The first words out of your mouth get the entire audience with you for the rest of the talk.

That's possible in every skill area. Never say, "I'm a little bit nervous about this." You eliminate nervousness simply by preparing until you have no nerves at all.

The Most Valuable Player

Look around at work and ask, "Who are the highest paid and most valuable people in this company? Who are the people that

You can eliminate all nervousness simply by preparing until you have no nerves at all.

everyone looks up to? Who gets paid the most and has their own private parking spot and drives a new car and who is paid more than we are? What do they offer that I don't? What skill do they have? What did they do for the company?"

Companies are very selfish. They will pay you more and more in order to have the pleasure of your services so you don't go somewhere else. It's really easy to get a raise. Just become good at what you do. They will run at you and thrust money in your hand and say, "Please, please, take more money. Stay here. Have better working conditions, because you contribute so much more to the company than you cost."

That's the key. They say that every person must contribute $3 to $6 in income or value or profit for every dollar they cost in terms of salary and wages. So keep increasing the amount of contribution that you make. Earl Nightingale had a wonderful question, which formed my life forever: "What can I do to increase the value of my contribution to my company today?"

If you want to be successful, accept responsibility—no excuses, no someday. Then say, "How can I increase my contribution? How can I contribute more? What additional skills can I offer?"

Go to your boss and ask, "How can I increase the value of my contribution to this company today? How can I do more, put more in, and keep looking for ways to do more?" You're in a world where 80 percent of people are looking for ways to do less. You will shoot past those people.

Create a Filing System

They say a cluttered desk is the sign of a cluttered mind. People today spend as much as 40 or 50 percent of their time looking for things. They allow them to pile up in stacks and get lost in drawers; then, when it's time to work, they have to spend a lot of time looking for these things. They find that they are missing one piece of information. Maybe it's a critical piece, so they have to stop the entire working process to look for it.

As I mentioned earlier, great military leaders will plan and organize and bring together every single resource. They'll check and double-check and triple-check to make sure they have everything before they launch the attack. They're ready for anything that can happen.

Make it a habit to bring together everything that you'll need to do the job. Clean up your workspace so that it's completely uncluttered. Organize what you need to do with an ordered checklist. Then start with number one: you put your head down, and you hit it. You work nonstop until that task is done.

The first time you do this, you're going to be distracted. You're going to find it hard to concentrate, but as you do it, it becomes easier and easier, and you become happier and happier. You become more elated. You have more energy.

I'll always come out of my office at home cheerful from the surge of endorphin that you get from completing a task, even a small one—putting the groceries away so your counter is clean, putting all your dishes away, mowing your lawn. Completing tasks with a beginning, a middle, and an end elates you and makes you feel positive and happy. It makes you eager to do

---

**One of the greatest productivity principles:
If a task can be done in less than 10 minutes,
do it immediately and get it out of the way.**

---

more work. You also start to earn the esteem of everybody around you.

One of the greatest productivity principles I ever learned was from a man who became the president of two Fortune 500 companies. He said if a task can be done in less than ten minutes, do it immediately, and get it out of the way.

If the task is going to take longer, set priorities on it. Get it organized. If it's going to take two or three hours, cut that chunk of time aside. Then work on that task 100 percent of the time.

Remember, your success in life will be determined by the value of your contribution, by your productivity, by the amount of work that you finish, and the value and the quality of the work that you do. If you are always working on high-value tasks and getting them done quickly and well, you're going to have a fabulous life; if you are not, no one can help you. There's no amount of politics that you can practice in an organization that's going to move you ahead if you are not completing your most important tasks and completing them quickly.

Prime Time

The final main idea for this chapter is, do important work during prime time. Why is that important?

Today you are a knowledge worker. This is Peter Drucker's wonderful contribution to management theory: you work with your mind, with your ability to function, to calculate and process information. Your brain requires a particular type of energy, and there is a time of day when you are best rested, most wide awake, and sharpest. That's when you do really important tasks, because you'll do them properly, you'll make fewer mistakes, you'll get more of them done, and you'll be more successful.

Many people have to go back and repeat a task because they made mistakes. I learned this very early in my career, when I was in a hurry. I got a digit out of place in a proposal that my boss asked me to prepare for one of the partners. The digit totally transformed the economics of the project. My boss looked at it and said, "With these economics, we cannot even be in this business relationship with these people." He took it to another person, and said, "Will you check these numbers again?"

This man, who was very meticulous, checked the numbers. He went back to my boss and said, "Brian made an important mistake here. He got this digit in the wrong place." Instead of a 15 percent return on investment, I had written down 1.5 percent, and he showed that the return would be 15 percent. This made it a very good investment for the company.

My boss took me aside, pointed this out to me, and said, "This could have been a major problem for us." I never made that mistake again. I always check and double-check. I always slow down, focus, and concentrate on these critical numbers, so that I don't get myself or my company into a serious problem.

Do your most important work during *prime time*.
Prime time is that period of time during the day
when you are freshest in mind and body.

I have now done hundreds of millions of dollars of real estate development. I've done shopping centers, office buildings, industrial centers, and several subdivisions. I've also advised many clients in these areas and made or saved them hundreds of millions of dollars. After that first mistake, I never again failed to do my most important work when I was at my most alert and most prepared.

According to every single study that's been done, the great majority of people are at their best in the morning, after sleeping. Some people say, "I'm good in the afternoon, I'm good in the evening," but the fact is, by that time you're tired. You're a little bit burned out. You're worn out. You're moving to Someday Island. "Tomorrow I'll do this. Next week I'll do that."

Many people think, "I'm too tired to do it this week." If you're tired, one of the best things you could do is stop working completely and get lots of rest. Take a weekend off, sleep in—eight, nine, ten hours. Take a nap, lie around like a vegetable, and just let yourself go, because sometimes it takes two or three days to recharge if you've gotten burned out from big projects or big jobs. Discipline yourself *not* to work for two or three days. When you start back to work again, your batteries will be fully charged, and you will accomplish vastly more in a day than you might accomplish in a week if you were tired out.

Air Travel

When you're traveling by air, there's a lot of wasted time. There's the drive to the airport, the wait, the flight, and the time to get to the hotel on the other end. If you don't use that time productively, you could lose several days of productivity, especially if you're traveling internationally.

How do we deal with this time? We go back to our old friend—preparation. In air travel, I travel about 100 to 200 days a year. At my peak, I was basically in the air all the time. I've traveled to 126 countries. I've gone back and forth over the Atlantic and the Pacific so many time I can't even count them. I get onto a Lufthansa flight out of Los Angeles for Frankfurt, and I know the names of all the flight attendants, and they know me, because I've flown so many times.

Before you fly, plan your flight, and look upon it as an opportunity to get a lot of uninterrupted work done. I often fly late in the day, so I arrive in the morning. You can't do serious brain work overnight, but you can read and catch up on subjects of medium complexity. You're not going to be able to do detailed reports, but you can read. I can read three hours a day or more, sometimes eight, because I organize my reading. When I sit down, I put my materials out, and then I read most of the time.

Again, a lot of it has to do with habit. Many people who fly do so rarely, and they look upon flying as a kind of holiday: "Wow, I'm going on a vacation. I sit there, and they bring me meals, and they have movies." But I look upon this as an opportunity to get a lot of uninterrupted work done, so I don't watch the movies. I don't waste time listening to music. I get on the plane, I read, and I learn.

When I went to Germany in 1994, I got up at the end of a business meeting, and I gave a talk in German. My sponsor said, "If you could speak German, we could create a million-dollar business around you here in Germany."

I said, "OK," and I began to study German. I got audio programs, I got books, I got a teacher. From then on, as I traveled back and forth, I spent the whole time studying, and within a year, I was speaking competent German. It took me much longer to be able to speak university German, but now I've given detailed forty-five- and sixty-minute business talks without translation or help.

I also speak French and Spanish. Then, when I started to speak a lot in Russia, I began to study Russian, which is a very difficult language, but I would use flying time as language learning time. I speak Portuguese and can get along quite well in Brazil. I speak Italian and get along quite well in Italy. I also started studying Chinese when I was going to China on a regular basis, and I could get by in Chinese. Chinese and Russian are extraordinarily complex languages, but it's just a matter of hours.

Rather than waste the time, I wanted to end up where I could ask questions and understand answers and order food in foreign countries. It's just a matter of plugging away, studying, taking notes, underlining, and writing things down.

When you start to study a language, it's like someone running through a darkened house and turning on all the lights. You activate more and more of your highest-functioning brain cells, and you actually become smarter and smarter.

The Art and Science of Meetings

With meetings, the first rule of law is, again, preparation. Make a list of everything you want to cover in the meeting.

The second rule is to circulate an agenda to everybody who's going to attend outlining the subjects you're going to discuss.

The third rule is to tell each person what they will be expecting to contribute: "We want you to be able to speak intelligently or answer questions on this subject."

Hold the meeting at a specific time—both a specific starting time and a specific ending time: the meeting is going to be at 10:00, and it will end at 10:50 sharp.

At 10:00, lock the door. One of the most challenging things in the world of work is excusitis. People come into the meeting late, so they miss the first five or ten minutes, when the most important subjects are laid out. Then you have to stop the whole meeting.

I learned this from a man who started off selling used cars and became the second-richest man in Canada. When he started a sales meeting, he locked the door. If you weren't there, you had to wait outside, and you'd better be there early next time. Nobody was ever late twice.

So lock the door, and don't let latecomers in. Assume that they are not coming at all. Never wait for latecomers; that's another big time waster. You say, "I'm sure so-and-so will be here soon. He's on the phone." Assume the latecomer is not coming at all, and begin immediately on time.

Start with the most important items first, so if you run out of time, it's on the least important items. In a staff meeting, for example, I go around to each person and have each one make a contribution. "Please tell us what you are doing. How is it going? What are your plans for the immediate future, and what help can we give you to be more effective?" We go from person to person. Some people have a lot to contribute; some have little. When I started calling on people who'd never been called on before, within two or three weeks, they came prepared; they contributed, and they asked questions.

The next stage was to revolve the chairmanship at the meeting: "Here's the meeting: it's all planned and laid out, and Camille or Bill is going to chair it today." At first, when I told them they were going to be running the meeting, people were very nervous, but then what did they do? They prepared. When they came, they were ready. They handed out the minutes and the agendas, and they made sure that they had information. They were amazingly responsible.

Meetings are one of the most wonderful tools for staff development. You can help to make your staff better and better by engaging them in contribution, asking for their opinions, putting them in charge of meetings, and giving them responsibilities for follow-up.

Then, five or ten minutes or five minutes before the meeting ends, say, "We're going to be wrapping up now. Is there anything else that we need to cover that we can't cover at a later time?" People will hurry up, and they'll say, what about this or what about that? Great. At the exact time of the end, you say, "OK, we're all done. See you next time."

Next, immediately circulate the minutes of the meeting. Write down what the meeting was, what you discussed, what you decided, and what each person has agreed to do. Hand out the minutes within twenty-four hours, so everybody has a copy of everything you discussed. Your chances of having everything done in that meeting goes up by ten times when everybody has the minutes from the meeting.

Otherwise, it's just an exercise of tossing around ideas and possibilities. Everyone leaves and goes back to doing what they were doing before with no sense of accountability. A meeting that does not end with specific assignments and deadlines for what each person is going to do is not really a meeting, it's a useless conversation.

I developed a technique that I use in my own meetings. I'll bring a glass or cup with a spoon in it. People say, "We should do this, and we should do that. Why don't we do this?"

I'll take the spoon, and I'll go tinkle, tinkle, tinkle. This means, who is going to put the bell on the cat's tail? Who exactly is going to do this? Yes, it's a good idea; your suggestion is very valuable. Who's going to do it? It's amazing how many people stop saying, "Someone should do this, and we should do that."

Always ring the bell, but remember that a meeting that ends without a clear, agreed-upon set of responsibilities for tasks that are to be done, when they're to be done, and how they're to be measured is not a meeting. It's merely a useless conversation. It does not motivate people. It demotivates people.

Rules for holding organized and productive meetings:

1. Preparation
2. Circulate an agenda to all attendees
3. Tell each person what they will be expected to contribute
4. Identify a specific time and length for the meeting, and start on time, regardless of who is in the room.
5. Lock the door and don't let latecomers in.
6. Start with the most important/critical items first.
7. Revolve the chairmanship of the meeting.
8. Announce meeting wrap up with 10 minutes left in the meeting.
9. Circulate minutes of the meeting to all attendees with follow-ups.

Go for the Touchdown

To repeat an important point: you can only move ahead in your career to the degree to which you get things done and you start and complete important tasks. With everything you do, you have that in your mind. Ask, what can I do that will increase the value of my contribution to my company? That becomes your organizing principle. The more you can contribute value to your company, the more successful you're going to be.

One decision that changed my life came when I was in my early thirties. As I mentioned before, I went to work for a big boss. Whenever I didn't have something that filled my time, I would go to him and say, "I'm all caught up. I want more responsibility."

"OK, great," he would say. "I'll think about that. I'll get back to you." He was swamped with work. He was running hundreds of millions of dollars' worth of businesses.

Before I had finished with that company, I was earning more than they had ever paid anybody in their history. I got more done, and I was more successful, starting from nothing, with no contacts or experience with a large company, just from saying one thing: "Give me more responsibility. I want more responsibility."

When you get that responsibility, take it like a pass in a Super Bowl game and run for a touchdown. Complete that task as fast as you can. Work on that task as though your future depended upon it, because it does.

As soon as you get the task done, like a dog that catches a stick and comes running back, say, "I want more. Throw the stick again. I want more responsibility." When they give it to you, take it, run with it, get it back, and do it quickly and well.

Chapter Five

The 10 Best Productivity Methods

In this chapter, I want to offer a treasure trove of the best productivity methods that I've ever taught. I'll covering them one by one.

The 80/20 Rule

Number one: *apply the 80/20 rule to everything.* The 80/20 rule was discovered by an Italian economist named Vilfredo Pareto in 1895. He found that 80 percent of the wealth in Italy seemed to be in the hands of 20 percent of the people. He then found that this was true for every country throughout Europe. Furthermore, 80 percent of the wealth in any industry was in the hands of 20 percent of the companies or organizations in that industry. He then found that 80 percent of the value of anything that you do is contained in 20 percent of the tasks.

The 80/20 Rule regarding productivity: 80% of the value of anything you do is contained in 20% of the tasks.

With the 80/20 rule, when you organize your time, 20 percent of what you do will account for 80 percent of the value of your contribution. As I've said, the most important thing you can do is to use your mind efficiently, which means to think. Stop and think. Time out. Make a list of everything you have to do, and then ask yourself, what 20 percent of activities on this list account for 80 percent of the value?

Peter Drucker said that sometimes it's the 90/10 rule: if you make a list of ten things that you have to accomplish, one of them will be worth more than all the other nine put together. If you're working on an item of low value, you can do an absolutely fabulous job, but it will be a waste of time. In fact, working on low-value items sabotages your career. You could be a hard worker, but it's what you're working on that's important. If you're a hard worker, and you're working on tasks that contribute the greatest value, you are going to be promoted faster and paid more.

The A-B-C-D-E Method

This is a wonderful technique, and I don't know where it comes from, but I've had many people who have read my books and attended my courses and say that this made them rich. This was the most incredible skill that they ever found, and they use it all the time.

When I speak in foreign countries, I call it the 1-2-3-4-5 method, because sometimes the alphabet not the same. In any case, this method says that A is something that you must do. The most important word in determining priorities is *consequences*. What are the consequences of doing this or not doing this task? Are they small, or are they large?

The most important tasks, the most valuable tasks are the ones for which the consequences are the most severe. An A task is something that has severe consequences. It's very important. It's something that you must do. If you don't, there's going to be trouble.

Always find out what things have the greatest potential consequences. Those become your A tasks. (We're assuming, of course, that by this time you have a list of tasks that you have written out before you begin.)

Your next task is your B task. A B task is something that you *should* do. It's getting back to your boss or your coworker or following up on correspondence. It's important because it has consequences, but the consequences are not as big as those of your A task.

What if you have more than one A task? That's all right. Then you prioritize them as A1, A2, and A3. The first task that you should do, which is the most important, is the one that has the greatest possible consequences. If you have more than one B task, you write B1, B2, B3. Here's the rule: never do a B task if an A task is left undone. If you have not completed your A tasks, if you're having the temptation to make excuses or to go to Someday Isle, stop yourself and get back to your A task.

Forcing yourself to think like this makes you a very intelligent person. It's almost like muscle building. What happens when you work out with weights? You pump blood into your muscles. That engorges your capillaries with fresh, oxygenated blood and causes your muscles to swell. If you do this on a regular basis and rest, the muscles relax, but they remain bigger. I call it the Schwarzenegger effect. Arnold Schwarzenegger has been going to gyms for four or five hours a day, five or six days a week, for fifty years. He still works out every day to keep those muscles pumped. This form—setting priorities and working on them—is mental muscle building. It makes you smarter.

A C task is something that's nice to do, but it has no consequences. Checking with your friends, going out for lunch, reading the paper, checking spam email—these are nice to do. These are almost recreational activities at work. It takes you back to school, when you played with your friends. When you go to work, you have a natural conditioning from childhood to see your coworkers as your friends, and you play with them. You chat with them, look at their emails, send them emails, and send them cartoons and jokes.

I have a good friend who's retired now. He sold out his interest in a large national business for many millions of dollars, and he bought condominiums, one in Hawaii and one in Florida. He lives a wonderful life, and he has lots of time on his hands. He's very friendly and very smart. Every day or two, you get a joke, a cartoon, a poem from him that he's picked up on the Internet or Facebook. That's all he does, because he's retired. He's still sending little jokes and stories to his playmates.

A C task is something that's nice to do, but don't do any C tasks until you've completed your A and B tasks. Human beings naturally tend to follow the law of least resistance. I call it the *expediency principle*. People do what is fun and easy rather than what is hard and necessary. The C tasks are things that are enjoyable and fun and easy. They give you a sense of pleasure, but whatever you do repeatedly over and over soon becomes a habit. Most people, the bottom 80 percent, fail because they get into the habit of doing things that are fun but contribute no value at all.

A D task in the A-B-C-D-E method is something that you delegate to someone else. Now here's the rule with delegation. You ask, "How much do I earn per hour from my work?" If you earn X number of dollars per year, you divide this amount by the number 2,000, which is the average number of hours that a person in our society works. In Germany, it's 1,800, and in France it's 1,600. In other countries it's less. These countries are less productive, so they have lower standards of living.

Anyway, you work about 2,000 hours. That's how you determine your hourly rate. If you make $100,000 a year, divide it by 2,000; that's $50 an hour. Then you ask, "Is there anything that I'm doing that does *not* pay $50 an hour? Would I pay someone else $50 an hour to do what I'm doing right now?" If you earn $50,000 a year, you earn $25 an hour: 2,000 into $50,000. You keep asking, "Is what I'm doing right now worth $25 or $50 an hour?" If it's not, stop doing it immediately, and do things that pay $25 or $50 an hour or more.

One of your jobs in life is to make your time worth more and more. A good friend of mine owns a law firm in Hollywood that has 105 lawyers, all of whom report to him. He told me about of his partners. He was a corporate lawyer; he worked with companies to draw up contracts. After he got out of law school, he earned $150 an hour. He was quite competent. Over time, he earned $175, and then $200 an hour.

Being in Hollywood, he noticed that more and more companies were getting into agreements where digital rights were part of the contract. His clients asked him, "Could you put something in this contract that protects our digital rights?"

"OK," he said, and he checked the law books to find out how to do it. He found that every lawyer in Los Angeles was asked to work on digital rights, but nobody specialized in it. So he decided to specialize in digital rights for companies in the entertainment industry. He worked on weekends, took additional courses, and traveled across the country to attend lectures and courses by the top experts on digital rights. He eventually pulled ahead, and his hourly rate went up to $250 and then $275.

In law, the most important thing is billable hours. How many hours can you sell as a lawyer? How many billable hours do you have? You want to have about 1,500 to 1,800 billable hours a year. The rest is flex time, travel time, and so on.

Today my friend charges more than $1,000 per billable hour for putting together big contracts with companies like Sony and Disney. They pay him that amount because he is so good, and his work is so good, that they can trust him to make sure that the agreement is to the benefit of all parties. Why get another lawyer to come in?

Sometimes my friend will bid $1 million to do the legal work for a major merger or transaction. They will happily pay that amount, because he will save them five and ten times as much. He understands the complexities of what each little phrase or paragraph will mean, or what this additional right will mean.

He saves his clients a fortune, and they come back and hire him over and over. At the beginning he was earning what lawyers earn when they start off—$100 or $150 an hour. Today he's one of the highest-paid lawyers in the world, and he's fully booked three to five years in advance. People will line up and will pay him anything he wants, because he's taken the time to become very good at something that has tremendous consequences.

To get back to the point, how do you delegate? You delegate everything that you can possibly delegate that someone else can do who works for a lower hourly rate than you do. You don't make coffee, you don't make photocopies, and you don't go to the Starbucks and get coffee for the gang. That doesn't pay $25 or $50 an hour. You wouldn't pay someone else that kind of money to do that.

Instead, make sure that you're doing work that pays more than you're getting today. If you do, you'll soon be paid more than you're getting today. So delegate everything you possibly can.

Always ask these questions: (1) Does this have to be done? (2) Does it have to be done now? (3) Does it have to be done by me? If it doesn't have to be done at all, if it doesn't have to be done by you, or if it can be done by someone else, delegate the task.

Business Model Reinvention

The last letter, E, is for *eliminate*. There is an entire movement called *reengineering*, which I have incorporated into my teachings. I have a program called "Business Model Reinvention." It forces you to go through every single part of your business and find out whether it is still relevant to building and maintaining a high-profit business. That means stopping and starting different things in your business. Reengineering means eliminating things that are no longer as valuable as they were at one time.

Our greatest enemy is the comfort zone. We become comfortable doing things in a certain way, even if that way is no longer very productive, and even if we know that there are better ways to do it. We continue because it's easy. It's the expediency factor: we do things that are fun and easy. In reality, what we should be doing is eliminating it.

So I ask my corporate clients, "Is there anything that you're doing today that, knowing what you now know, you would not start doing again today?" If they say, "I would not start this up, I would not get into this, I would not do this anymore," then the next question is, "How do you get out, and how fast?"

The rule is that if you would not start doing it again today, then doing it is a total waste of time. It means that you're basically wasting your time, wasting your life, and you're hurting your career.

Therefore the first thing I do when I work with a company is walk them through all their products, services, organization, and distribution systems. I have them put a frame over these things and ask, "If we were not doing this today, knowing what we now know in terms of results, in terms of productivity, would we get into it?" If the answer is no, the next question is, "How do we get out, and how fast?" This is called *zero-based thinking*.

Your courage and ability to do that can change your life. Every company that I've worked with, without exception, has areas of activity that they shouldn't be in. At one time these areas were good and profitable, but today the market has changed, and they're not anymore.

The A-B-C-D-E Productivity Method:

- **A** tasks are something you absolutely must do.
- **B** tasks are something that you *should* do
- **C** tasks are something that would be nice to do, but not doing it has no meaningful consequences. (Checking spam e-mail, reading the paper)
- **D** tasks are something you delegate to someone else. (Those tasks that are worth considerably less than your hourly rate)

    Three questions:
    1. Does this have to be done?
    2. Does is have to be done now?
    3. Does it have to be done by me?

- **E** tasks are something to eliminate entirely. "Reeingineering" your life or your business model means to eliminate things that are no longer as valuable as they were at one time.

Steve Jobs and the Gentleman

What is the most profitable company in the world? The answer is Apple. It's the first company in the world to have $1 trillion in the bank.

Everybody knows the story of Apple. Back in the eighties, they fired Steve Jobs. Steve Jobs was a very irritating person. He insulted people, he shouted them, and the company was on the verge of bankruptcy, so the board of directors voted him out. They brought in a senior executive in high-tech industry.

After another ten years, the company was on the verge of bankruptcy again, and Steve Jobs had been asked to come in and consult. They didn't give him all the information, but they gave him enough, and he gave some good advice as an outside consultant.

In the mid-nineties, they realized the company was on the verge of bankruptcy, so they brought in Steve Jobs, and they made him president again. All the other people, who had ruined the company, abandoned it. Steve Jobs asked, "How much money do we have in the bank?"

They had enough for about two and a half months, and then the company would have to close. They had more than 4,000 employees worldwide, but the company had two and a half months of cash, and the sales were not generating enough cash. They were on the verge of bankruptcy.

So Steve Jobs asked the zero-based thinking question: "Is there anything that I'm doing that I would not start doing again today?" He brought in several teams of managers and said, "I want you to go through all the products that we have, and give me what they are and how many we have."

Nobody knew how many products Apple had. It turned out that they had 104 products—big sellers, medium sellers, low sellers, no sellers. Steve Jobs said, "All right. I want you to go through this list in several teams, and I want you to give me the ten products that are the most profitable, the ones that we should focus all of our energies on."

In a week or two, they came back with lists of ten, and the lists were different. Some teams said, "Even though this is not profitable, we should keep up with it, because it has great potential or it was a great product in the past." Comfort zone.

> Apply *zero-based thinking* to your life or your business:
> Ask yourself, "Is there anything that you're doing today
> that, knowing what you know now, you would not start
> doing again today?" Whatever you answer, find a
> way to eliminate it from your life or your business.

Jobs went through it all, and then he handed out the list. He said, "I want you to take all of these lists and come back with just ten. Out of the 104 products, just ten that we can focus on."

The employees shouted and were upset. They said, "We can't do that. It's not possible. We're such a big company. There's so many people involved, so many people's ox will get gored if we discontinue these products."

Jobs said, "Either the products go, or you go."

So the managers came back, and they ended up with ten products out of 104. Then Jobs sent them out again. He said, "I want you to come back with four. We're going to focus just on four products." Of the 104, they came back with four products, and they abandoned the other products, which slowed down the cash drain that was killing them.

Then Steve Jobs did something very interesting. For all of his career, he had been badmouthing Bill Gates. He had always accused Microsoft of being a crummy company; it was uninspired, and its products were mediocre.

The companies had started off at the same time. They'd gone public at the same time. They'd grown rapidly at the same time. Then Microsoft exploded. It became a leading company in the world because of its business model, and Apple was on the verge of bankruptcy.

After insulting Bill Gates for at least ten years, Jobs called Gates, who took his call. He said, "Bill, I have a problem. I need a lot of cash, and I need it right away, or Apple is going to go broke."

You know what Bill Gates said? "Steve, we've had a lot of differences of opinion in the past, but Apple is too important a company to go broke. I'll give you the money you need."

"I'll pay you any interest rate," said Jobs.

"No," said Gates, "I won't lend you the money. I'll buy stock in Apple. I'll go in with you. I'll buy stock in Apple, so if Apple is successful, then I'll be successful. If it's not, then we will both suffer." He bought a huge chunk of Apple.

Apple took that money, turned the company around completely, and made it the most valuable company in the world. You can just imagine what Bill Gates's Apple stock is worth today—billions and billions of dollars. But you can also see what a gentleman he was. He said, "Even after all these insults, your company is too important to go out of business." He saved Apple at the critical moment.

At any rate, this is an example of zero-based thinking: eliminating every single product that is not as good as the others. It isn't even that they aren't good products. It's that you can't do everything, so you have to cut back. All over the world, I teach thousands of business owners business model reinvention: you sit down, and you evaluate every single product and every single activity you have, and you reinvent the company to turn it into a profit machine.

If you're not generating high levels of profits consistently in your business today, your business model is not working. It's obsolete. It's being replaced by the market and by your competition. If you're serious about success, you need a new business model. So let's sit down and look at the ingredients in the model like the pieces of a jigsaw puzzle. Which ones do we have to remove, and which ones do we have to replace? Then we put it all back together again.

I have helped business owners reinvent their companies a thousand times simply by standing back and eliminating all the low-value or no-value products and activities and transform the company into a profit machine.

According to Harvard, 80 percent of companies are using obsolete business models. Fully fifty-five business models that have been identified. Every company has a business model, but Harvard also discovered that even at the Fortune 500 level, the heads of companies are often not clear about their business model.

At most companies, if you say, "What is your business model?" they don't really know for sure.

"We produce this, and we sell that."

"How do you determine the products that you offer, and the companies that you sell to? How do you set your prices? How do you advertise and market and promote? How do you position yourself against competition?"

Your business model consists of ten different factors that go together like pieces of machinery that are screwed one into the next. If all the pieces are correct, the machinery works beautifully.

According to Harvard University 80% of companies are using obsolete business models.

Imagine that you have a piece of machinery that doesn't work, like an alarm clock. You take the clock apart, you lay out all the pieces on a workbench, you identify the defective piece or pieces, and you replace them with new, effective pieces. Then you put the clock back together again, and it works perfectly.

Every business is like a piece of machinery. In almost every case, one or two key components of the business model are broken or ineffective. They're not working. As a result, the company is struggling to earn profits. The business model is the profit model; therefore, you can tell if you have a good business model because you are making good profits, consistently, dependably, day by day, week by week, month by month.

If you're not, it's time to pull back on the reins, stop, and say, "Time out. Let's sit down and take a look at this carefully, part by part, and make sure that we're doing the right things. In what areas where are we not generating profits? What are we doing that we would not start again today if we had to do it over?"

A company is a profit-generating organism. Its whole purpose is to make a profit by providing customers with products and services that improve the quality of their lives.

I had dinner with economist Milton Friedman not long before his death. He said the purpose of a business is to generate a profit. It's not to do social or charitable work or to save the world. It is to produce products and services that enrich the lives of people and to do it in a profitable way, whereby you generate more than you spend.

Peter Drucker said that profits are the cost of the future. Where there are no profits, there is no future for that business or that industry, or sometimes for that whole country.

> **When it comes to productivity, you must think of yourself like a business: You are a profit-generating mechanism. Your goal is to become productive enough so you can generate a higher income to become financially independent.**

As an individual, you are also a profit-generating mechanism. You earn money, and your goal is to earn more money than it costs you to live. There's no point in earning just enough so you can eat. You want to have more than that. You want to generate higher income. You want to save and accumulate money. You want to become financially independent, and then you want to become wealthy. So you have a personal business model as well. Of course, your personal business model follows exactly along the same lines as a corporate business model. What service do you offer? What do you charge, and how could you improve your service so you could charge more? What could you do differently? What could you add or subtract? What could you start doing or stop doing? These are all important questions. They force you to think, and thinking makes you smarter.

Then ask who your competition is. Who are the other people who are doing similar work to you who want to earn the same amount of money or more? The results of your work have to be better than theirs for you to be paid more than them.

All of these questions force you to ask, "How can I do things better? How can I be better? How can I as a person create a personal business model that will end up in me becoming rich?"

You don't want to have enough to pay your bills. You don't even want to be well-off. You want to be rich. You may not become rich, but don't fail to become rich because you never set it as a goal. Set it as a goal, and then say, "How can I do this? What do I need to do more of or less of to be able to make a greater contribution so that I can earn more money, so that I can create a better life for myself and my family?" These are all critical parts of productivity.

Fully 50 percent of working time is wasted in nonproductive activities. In some cases, it's 60 or 70 percent. In every workplace, everyone knows who's the most productive. You don't have to wear a sign on your back. Everybody knows who the most valuable person is. In a business, if you have ten people, two of those people produce 80 percent of the results. Those people have every door open to them. They are revered by their management. Many companies are built around the talents of one or two people.

A friend of mine wrote a book some years ago called *The Outperformers*. It said that every company is successful because it has at least one outperformer. Small companies have to have at least one person who is extremely productive. If the company is a sales organization, it has to have at least one super salesperson.

A perfect example is Hewlett-Packard. Hewlett-Packard started off with two guys that came out of the Navy. They started a high-tech company, and they came up with an idea for a machine. Hewlett was a tremendous engineer. He came up with a simple machine that went into a lot of other machines, and they started producing it in a garage in Palo Alto, California. That was the start of Silicon Valley. It's on the bus route. You can drive by, and you'll see a big sign saying this is the garage where Hewlett-Packard started so many years ago.

Become an *outperformer*—become known as the person who produces results.

David Packard was a great personality, a wonderful sales-man. He could sell like an artist, so he went out and sold the product. Because he could sell the product, and Bill Hewlett could design and manufacture it, they created one of the most successful companies in history.

Apple started with Steve Jobs and Steve Wozniak. Micro-soft was started by Bill Gates and his partner. In every case, one was the technical genius; the other one was the marketing genius. The other one knew what customers wanted and how to make customers happy. The other one knew how to produce the product.

It's the same thing with you. You have to have an out-performer, and if you don't, I have a suggestion for you: Become an outperformer. Become known as the person that really pro-duces results. Maybe you'll have to work a little harder and stay a little later and come a little earlier, maybe you'll have to read and study and take courses, but throw your whole heart into becom-ing so valuable that they will pay you anything to keep you.

The Law of Three

Let me turn to the law of three. I discovered it after years and years and years of working in the area of time management and personal productivity.

I put all of my students through this exercise. I tell them to make a list of everything they do in the course of a week or a month. I usually have them complete it before they come to my program for the first day. They bring it with them, and people will write down ten or twenty things. Some people will write down thirty or forty. Some have fifty or sixty.

When they bring the list, I'll say, "Without looking at your list, I can tell you that 10 percent of the things that you do on that list are worth 90 percent of all the others, 90 percent of the things that you do are primarily time wasters, and there are three things that you do that are worth more than all the others put together."

How do you identify the three? You ask three magic questions. These questions will make you rich. If I only had five minutes to tell people how to become rich, this is what I would tell them.

1. If I could only do one thing all day long, which one activity would contribute the greatest amount of value to my work and to my company? You take some time to think about it, but most people will know the answer almost immediately. In some cases it's very easy. If I could just close sales; if I could just prospect better and get to talk to better prospects.

   There are several parts of selling. Usually it's just one link in the chain that either makes you a superperformer, an outperformer, or a failure.

   Once you have the answer, put a circle around that one activity. Then you ask:

2. If I could only do *two* things on this list all day long, what would be the second most valuable thing that I could do?

   This is a little bit harder, by the way. Number one is usually quite easy. Number two is more difficult, but you'll figure it out quite quickly. Then you ask:

3. If I could only do three things on this list all day long, which would be the third most valuable thing that I could contribute to my business?

If you look at those three and stand back, it'll suddenly hit you almost like a flashbulb going off in your face. It'll hit you that these three things will determine your entire financial results in life. They determine your success and your happiness. They determine your levels of accomplishment and your levels of respect and esteem. Everything comes down to those three things. The other 97 percent contribute very little value at all.

The law of three says put the others apart. Pick numbers one, two, and three. Go to work on number one, and do only number one until you have done everything that you possibly can in that area. Then, go to number two, and go to number three. Every day of your life, ask yourself, "What are my big three?"

For several years, Warren Buffett was the richest man in the world. Today he's worth about $84 billion. If you had bought stock in his company for $100 when he started it, Berkshire Hathaway, it would worth more than $2 million today, because its value has increased 25 percent or more interest per annum for year after year and decade after decade.

When they asked Buffett, "What's your secret to success?" He said, "My secret is simple. I just say no to everything. I say no to everything except my three most important tasks, and I only work on those three tasks. I do them all day long, and I spend the rest of my time studying."

He reads 500 pages a day. He studies and reads books and articles six to eight hours each day, and he only spends about two hours a day doing the big three. He delegates or eliminates everything else.

I have a good friend who was with IBM for twenty-five years. IBM got into serious financial problems in the late eighties and early nineties. They thought the company was going to go bankrupt. They fired the president and all the top executives. They brought in a new president, who brought in new people and turned the company around.

One thing they found was that many people in the company, who were very talented, were doing many things that were of low or no value. They brought in the law of three. Every person in the company was schooled in identifying the three most important things they did all day long, and then working on those three all the time.

Managers were schooled in helping each employee to keep focus on the big three. If a manager was talking to people or meeting with members of the staff, the first thing he would ask is, "What are your big three?"

The person had to know it absolutely, crystal clear like a switchblade—wham, wham, wham. Then the manager would ask, "Is what you're doing right now one of those three?" The company turned around.

One of the biggest and best corporate turnarounds in the history of the world was the IBM turnaround, based on identifying each person's big three and encouraging each person to get better and better at doing those three tasks. This is enough in itself to make you a great success.

Practice the *Law of Three*:

1. Make a list of every task and/or activity that you do over the course of a week.
2. If I could do one thing, all day long, which one task would contribute the greatest amount of value to my work and company?
3. If I could do two things, all day long, what would be the second most valuable task that I could do?
4. If I could do three things, all day long, what would be the third most valuable task that I could do?

These are your Big Three that will contribute 80% of more of the value to your life and business. Go to work on them right away, one by one.

Upgrade Your Key Skills

The fourth productivity method is to upgrade your key skills. This is the natural follow-through from the law of three. Once you've identified the three tasks, you devote yourself to becoming better and better at each of them. You want to become the best there is in those three tasks.

The lawyer I mentioned earlier realized that the most valuable thing he could do was to write complex intellectual agreements that dealt with all of the components of high-tech and deliver them to his clients to save and earn them enormous amounts of money. He could charge almost anything for that, because these companies were dealing with billions of dollars of assets that could be affected by contractual clauses.

So identify your three big tasks, and decide that you're going to become the best.

One of the best affirmations that you can use, which I started using with my children when they were young is, "I'm the best. I'm the best. I'm the best." You just keep saying that over and over again. I tell my kids, "You're the best. You are so good at what you do. You are really excellent."

I tell my staff the same thing. My secretary, Shirley, started off very shy, with very low self-esteem, a very bad self-image. I would tell her, "You know, you're the best. You're the best." She worked with me for many years. By the time she was finished, she would say, "I'm the bomb. I'm the best in this business," and she meant it. She was happy, and she was smiling. She did wonderful work. I complimented her and praised her over and over, and she got better and better at all the key things she did.

Leverage Your Special Talents

The fifth productivity method is leveraging your special talents. Leverage and multiply. That means teach other people how to do the most important things that you do so you can get more and more of those things done within your company.

When I started one of my companies, my greatest contribution was that I could sell. The greatest way I could leverage my sales ability was to recruit people who were eager to be successful and then teach them how to sell.

When I was twenty-four, I got a job in sales, and I finally learned how to sell. I sold so well that they asked me if I would like to recruit people; they would give me an override on my sales. So I began to run newspaper ads with my own money offering a highly paid sales job. People in six countries came to me. I would interview them. If I liked them, I would hire them and train them how to sell.

Every month I would work with one of my sales teams in those six countries. I kept traveling and teaching and taking them out and going out with them on sales calls. I made them all really great salespeople.

My income went up ten and twenty and thirty times because of my overrides from their sales. I kept in touch people on my teams with over the years. Many of them have gone on to become millionaires, heads of conglomerates, and owners of companies. The turning point in their lives came when I began to leverage myself by teaching them to become very good at what I was doing.

**Leverage your talent by teaching it well to others
in your company, and multiply it's effects.**

Identify Your Key Constraints

The sixth idea is to identify your key constraints. The idea of constraint management and constraint removal comes from a professor at the University of Tel Aviv named Eliyahu Goldratt He wrote a book called *The Goal*, and in it he introduced a method of looking at work that has had an enormous impact.

It's called the *theory of constraint*. They have three-day seminars on it. The theory of constraint is one of the most brilliant time management principles I've ever seen, and every top business-person I know has immersed themselves in it.

The theory of constraint basically says this: between you and any goal that you want to achieve, there is one major con-straint. There's one major factor that determines how fast you achieve that goal, and your job is to identify that factor, and then to eliminate the constraint. That will move you toward your goal faster than anything else you can do.

Goldratt also says that once you have removed a constraint, you will find another. Now your job is to eliminate this sec-ond constraint, which is now setting the speed at how quickly you achieve your most important goal or complete your most important activity.

A very simple example. Apple is selling laptop computers. The laptops are good, but the competitors are selling something that's pretty much equally good, and the competition is fierce, because now we have countries such as Japan and Taiwan and China producing computers at very low cost with very high lev-els of effectiveness.

Apple said, "We can't make it just with computers. We have to have something else. We need a new product that nobody has." So they thought and thought, and then they realized that people were carrying boom boxes so they could listen to audio-cassettes or CDs. Remember those?

Sony came up with Walkmans. With Walkmans, you could listen to cassettes and CDs and carry them around with you. But you could only carry a few pieces of music, a few songs, with you.

The *theory of constraint* says that between you and any goal that you want to achieve, there is basically one factor that determines how fast you achieve that goal.

Apple came up with a product with which you could put and record a whole series of songs onto one machine and play it with earphones. They came up with the iPod, and their marketing slogan was "1,000 songs in your pocket." You could have all your songs on one little gadget that fit in your pocket or your purse, and you could listen to them with earphones.

They priced iPods at $500, and they sold five million of them. Apple went from struggling on the verge of bankruptcy to being a profitable company. Again they said, "We have to have another product that nobody has, that is way beyond anything that anyone is doing."

There were lots of portable telephones at that time, and Motorola was king. Today Motorola is an afterthought in telephone technology. The biggest company in the world was Nokia. Nokia had 50 percent of the world market for portable phones. Nokia and Blackberry owned the world market for portable telephones. Nokia had 49 to 50 percent, and Blackberry had 30 to 40 percent; all the other companies shared the rest.

When Apple announced the iPhone, both of these competitors said it was a toy. It would never work; it was only of interest to teenagers and to children. Who wants to take pictures and send messages and make short movies that they can entertain their friends with? Who wants to take long lists of names and have email and everything? People don't want that. They just want a simple, technological item like a cell phone.

Within five years, both of those companies were bankrupt. They're gone. Nokia was taken over by Microsoft, which shut it down, but Blackberry just went bankrupt. They went from 50 percent of the world business market to less than one percent in five years. That made Apple one of the richest and most prosperous companies in the world.

Apple reevaluated their business model. They said, "We have to come up with something that is better and different from anything else out there," and they continually improved it. They had to price it so that everybody would buy it. They came up with the magic price of $500. In Europe and in Asia, it's €500—more or less the equivalent $700 or $800. Now it's $1,000, and it's even up to $1,500 if you get enough bells and whistles with it. It enabled Apple to assemble a trillion-dollar war chest.

Then Apple came out with the iPad, which decimated the market for desktop and the laptop computers.

Apple looked at brand-new ways of doing things. They experimented with brand-new products and pricing and customers and transformed the market.

Whatever business you're in today, it's going to be obsolete sooner or later. It may even be obsolete right now. So you're going to have to start thinking, "What is my next miracle? What am I going to have to be doing five years from now to earn the kind of money that I want to make?"

How do you identify the constraints to your productivity? You ask, "What is my most important goal in life, the goal that would have the greatest impact on my life if I could achieve it?" In business, it's a financial goal. Then you ask, "What sets the speed at which I achieve my goal?"

In sales, what sets the speed is the number of sales you make, but you can say, "What sets the speed at which I earn this amount of money in sales?" There's usually one thing you can focus on.

In your business, you can say, "What sets the constraints upon the growth of my business?" Many companies have found, and this goes back thirty or forty years, that almost always it is finding and hiring a person with a particular set of talents and skills—a champion, the person who can make this product successful.

Steve Ballmer went in and became the president of Microsoft very early in the game. He was one of the early employees; Steve Jobs liked him, and he was very competent. He has now sold out his interest. He's now retired, and he's one of the richest men in the world. I think he's worth $16 billion. Some of the richest people in the world are people who started with nothing and went to work with companies that grew rapidly. They grew with those companies, and they got stock options, or they bought stock in the company. As the company grew, they became wealthier and wealthier, like Warren Buffett.

There are Buffett billionaires all over the world. These are people who, at a very early age, started to buy stock in Warren Buffett's company, Berkshire Hathaway. They kept at their jobs. Some of them are lawyers, some are doctors, some are dentists, and some of them own small businesses, but throughout their lives, their investing strategy was to buy more stock in Warren's company.

These people are now billionaires and multibillionaires. You never see them on the lists of the big corporate chieftains. They're just stockholders who did what Warren Buffett said: buy a stock and never sell it. He said, "I buy stocks, and I never sell them. I buy good stocks, and I just let them grow through good times and bad." That's his one strategy: to buy good stocks, and never sell. It's made him the third-richest person in the history of the world.

Get Out of Technological Time Traps

Number seven is get out of technological time traps. Many companies have gone broke because they weren't able to move with modern technology. People don't realize that the technology that is succeeding with their competitors is brand-new, and what they have is obsolete. They have to get with the game. They have to bring in completely brand-new technology to stay alive. Every successful company is constantly upgrading its technology.

A company can get into a technological time trap by trying to make old technology work against new competitors, who have faster, better, cheaper, easier, and more compatible products and services. Because of the comfort zone, they keep trying to make old stuff work.

If you are trapped by old technology, if you do not have the ability or the will or the money to upgrade, you are working on borrowed time. This is not optional. You can't say, "Maybe I will, maybe I won't." If you are not as good as or better than your best competition, your time is almost over. Your business is almost finished.

As I've already mentioned, another technological trap is becoming tied up with emails. People are constantly working on their computers. My company (which I've actually sold to my partner) has thirty-eight people who work in high-tech mar-

---

Don't try to make old technology work against new competitors with better, faster, cheaper and more up-to-date technology. You are working on borrowed time.

---

keting. They are required to turn off their phones for most of the day. They also turn off their emails. They're required to turn off all this technology so that they can focus single-mindedly on the one thing that determines their success: selling more products and generating more sales.

As I've already pointed out, fully 50 percent of time spent in offices today is wasted. The number-one time waster is idle chit-chat with coworkers. The number-two time waster is going on and off your computer and email all day long. By the end of the day, what's happened? You're exhausted, and you haven't gotten anything done. So you take a trip to Someday Isle: "Tomorrow I'll do this. Next week I'll do that." Eventually that becomes your habit, and everybody knows how productive you are.

Slice and Dice the Task

The eighth idea is to slice and dice the task. It's a technique that's been developed by time management specialists. It means to take a large task and break it down into small pieces and do one thing at a time. There's that famous question, "How do you eat an elephant?" The answer is, one bite at a time. Remember the Henry Ford quote: "The biggest goal in the world can be achieved if you just break it up into enough small pieces, and then do one piece at a time, one step at a time."

That's the technique. You take a job, and you break it into a series of small pieces, because it's much easier to motivate yourself to do one small piece, even if it's just making a list of the pieces. That triggers you into taking the first constructive action. When you take the first constructive action, you get positive feedback: an endorphin rush, a feeling of happiness. You eagerly jump into tasks number two and number three, and pretty soon you're flying.

When people come in and ask if you have time for lunch, you say, "I can't go now. I'm going to finish up this task. I'm going to eat lunch at my desk." You start to think of all kinds of reasons you can't waste time because you have so many little things to complete.

Urgency

Most productive people have a sense of urgency. They move quickly on a task. They have an idea, and they act quickly on it. They are reading, and they come across an insight or a strategic principle, and they immediately take action. Stop, and do it now.

The most powerful words you can use are, "Do it now." Repeat these words over and over again, and you will impress them deeper and deeper into your subconscious mind. When you have a tendency to put off a task, say, "Wait a minute. "Do it now." You push yourself. You become your own cheerleader, and you motivate yourself to get started.

"Do it now" are wonderful words for a sense of urgency. When I was working with that big boss early in my career, nothing moved me up faster than starting and completing

---

**The most powerful words you can use to be
more productive are, "Do It Now!"**

---

everything he asked me to do. He had a whole office building
full of staff that he could turn a job over to, but if he wanted
it done quickly, he gave it to me. He said, "I can have a lot
of people do this work, but if I want it done fast, I give it to
Brian."

One day he came to me. He had sent me to Reno, to look
at a piece of property, along with two or three of the property
owners and a couple of people in our company. It was a multi-
million-dollar piece of property that overlooked Reno, and it
looked like a fabulous property for developing homes because
it had tremendous views. It was beautiful, it was green. They
had springs of water on it, and the owners wanted to sell it for
several million dollars.

The property looked great, and the person in charge went
back and told my boss that we should buy the property. He put
down a deposit of $1 million on it. Then my boss came to me
and said, "Brian, we've bought that property now, and we need
to develop it." He knew that he could send me in, and I would
start to put together the right contractors. I had developed an
ability to do that—making lists, making smaller lists, getting
started, and moving quickly. He said, "If you can get this project started, I'd appreciate it."

I immediately went down to Reno. I was living in Edmon-
ton, Alberta at that time, so the trip was about 1,000 miles. I
went to see the lawyer who was handling the transaction for
the owners who were selling the property. I said, "I'm here to

start the development of the property. Can you give me any advice?" The lawyer, a very nice guy, went silent. I said, "Is there a problem?"

He said, "Have you spoken to anybody about the development potential for this property?"

"No," I said. "I've done several real estate developments on flatter land, so I know how to develop a residential subdivision."

"Before you finalize everything, why don't you talk to someone who knows this property better than anyone else?"

It was a hydraulic engineer who lived in a small town about fifty miles from Reno. The lawyer said, "This guy can answer all your questions. He'll tell you anything you need to know about developing the property."

I had learned that one of the smart things to do is speak to really knowledgeable people, so I rented a car. It was wintertime. I drove through icy, snowy roads down to this little town. I found the engineer's home office, went in, and said, "I'm responsible for developing this property."

He was a really nice guy. He leaned back and he said, "Brian, you will never develop that property. There's no water on the property."

"Wait a minute," I said, and we had the maps and laid them all out. "When I went to the property, they showed me the water in these places."

"What they showed you was water that was on the property adjacent to the property they're selling you. This property has been on the market now for several years. In fact, there's a rumor going around Reno that the owners have found a sucker to buy the property, because once you buy the property, you will have a piece of land that they will not develop for 100 years."

"Really?"

"You don't need to quote me on this," he said, "but I did all the hydraulic engineering work on this property. There's no water there, and there never will be."

So I went back to the lawyer, who had our million-dollar check in his trust fund. We'd sent him the money, and my boss had instructed me to transfer it from the lawyer's trust fund to the sellers and close the transaction.

I went back to him, and said, "I want that check back."

He looked at me and said, "Thank God you found out. I have felt uncomfortable about being in the middle of this deal, knowing that this is a useless and undevelopable piece of property that they were trying to palm off on people from out of town."

The property was supposed to close that day. The $1 million was supposed to transfer from the lawyer's trust fund at 5:00. I walked into his office at five minutes to 5:00 and demanded that he return the check, and he wrote up a certified check. I'd arrived the night before. I'd been working and driving all day, and I caught the last plane home. On the way back, I phoned my boss and told him everything.

"I guess it was a good idea that you went down a day early," he said. "I wasn't planning for you to go down until maybe next week. Thank you for going earlier." He was rich because he was very thoughtful and careful about money. I walked into his office the next morning and gave him that check for $1 million.

From that day onward, I became one of the most valuable people in that company. I had my own office and my own staff, and I was in charge of large developments and companies, and it was the most amazing thing. If you wanted something done in this huge, multinational conglomerate, bring Brian in, almost like a hired gun.

I wrote a book called *Victory,* which describes major historical episodes in which small forces were able to win extraordinary victories and conquer empires. Over and over I found that a sense of urgency was the vital factor that enabled an outnumbered force to see an opening in the enemy's lines, and move fast and move now. If they had waited two hours, that opportunity would have closed, and they would have been defeated. They would have all been killed, and the war would have been lost.

Single-Handling Every Task

In today's technological world, where interruptions are coming from all directions, people are proud of themselves for being great multitaskers. "Boy, I can multitask with the best of them."

But all the research says the same thing: no matter who you are, you can only do one thing at a time. That's why I've always held that single-handling a task, with dedication and focus, is important.

Imagine trying to read and watch television at the same time. You shift your mind to the television, and then you shift it back to the reading. Try to be talking on the telephone and watching television at the same time. The human brain is structured so that it can do a thousand things in a row, but only one thing at a time.

What people call multitasking is really task shifting. Imagine you want to shoot a rifle at a target, and you have several targets. You can only shoot at one target at a time. You can't shoot at multiple targets. You may be able to shoot at several

---

**Research says that *multitasking* is a myth—
it is really *task shifting*.**

---

targets in a row, but you have to stop, aim, fire, stop, move, aim, fire. You may be able to do that quickly, but each time you have to stop and start again.

How does this work today? We stop a task, and we answer an email. This is the greatest interruption. Actually, the greatest interruption is other people. The biggest time wasters in the world of work are people who do not value their time highly and come and want to chat with you. They want to break up their monotony, because, after all, work time is playtime. They felt they've worked enough now—maybe a few minutes. It's time to play. It's time to ruin your career.

The people who are most harmful to your career are those who do not value your time. They are the biggest time wasters of all. They come and say, "Hi, do you have a minute?" Or, "I just saw this joke." Or, "Did you watch this on TV last night?"

It doesn't matter what it is; it's simply a reason or a method to waste your time. You have to learn to say no. You say, "I'd love to talk to you right now, but I'm really busy. I have to get this done."

Then you do one thing at a time, because of transition time. This is the time it takes for you to stop doing one task, shift to another task, and then start working on that task and getting that done.

I write four books a year. The average professional writer who works full time, who lives only for writing books, writes one every two to three years. How do I write so many books?

I learned that if you start working on a book, go and do something else, and then come back, you have to review everything that you've done up to that point. You have to get completely reorganized. You say, "What did I say? What did I not say? Where was I?" You have to start over again. Then you can begin working on the next chapter. If you stop, you have to go back and remind yourself of everything you've done so far before you can begin again. That's why I say it takes an average of seventeen minutes to return to a task. Sometimes it's not just seventeen minutes. Sometimes, once you digress or try to multitask, you stop working on that task altogether for the day or the week.

Sometimes I'll do a workbook, and the workbook will be enough work for a room full of businesspeople to work with for two full days. I'll take one or two days to write it. I will put my head down, turn off everything, and work nonstop. Maybe I'll check email once or twice a day, but I don't do any other tasks. I just focus. I concentrate. I work nonstop, and as a result, I get more done faster.

With this approach, it becomes easier and easier for you to do better and better work. You'll feel happier. You'll feel more in control of your life and your activities. You'll get more done, faster and of higher quality, than you can imagine right now. But you have to stop thinking about multitasking, because it does not exist. It is a fantasy. Human beings are incapable of multitasking.

It's true that you can drive a car and listen to the news on the radio, because that uses two completely different sensory inputs. You can drive the car, which requires physical inputs.

You can listen to the news, which is mental, or you think about your wife or family, which has to do with emotion. You can do things that require completely different parts of your brain, but you cannot do several different types of work at the same time. You can only do one.

If you do one task, and you start with your most important task, and you're completely organized, and you start to work through it using a checklist, and you stay at it until it's complete, you will accomplish ten times as much as the average person. Eventually you'll be paid ten times as much. You'll be so productive that people will want to pay you more.

As I said earlier, when my big boss sold his company, I got an offer from another big boss, who offered me triple what I had been earning. Later I asked him, "Why did you decide to hire me?"

"Because you have a reputation around town for getting an enormous amount of work done. My company is working on many projects. Different people are working on them, and nothing ever gets completed. I knew if I hired you, all these projects would get completed."

The first thing I did was to go through the company and fire half the people, because these were people who were multitasking, talking to their friends, chatting on the phone, and going for lunch. They were furious with me. It was a great storm, but I cleared out all the detritus, all the weak people who were wasting so much time, and I turned that company around. Hundreds of millions of dollars worth of properties were developed and factories and businesses were taken over, just by single focus.

Let me restate the methods we've gone over in this chapter.

The Ten Best Productivity Methods

1. Apply the 80/20 rule to everything.
2. Use the A-B-C-D-E method continually.
3. Use the law of three.
4. Upgrade your key skills.
5. Leverage your special talents.
6. Identify your key constraints.
7. Get out of technological time traps.
8. Slice and dice the task.
9. Develop a sense of urgency.
10. Single-handle every task.

If I were to highlight one method, I would say, make a list. Without a list, you're swimming in the air. Make a list and write down every one of your top ten goals, the first ten goals you can think of, and then ask yourself, "Which one of these goals, if I were to complete it, would have the greatest positive impact on my life?" Then put a circle around that and say, "What one activity could I engage in right now that would move me closer to the achievement of that goal?" and write that down.

Then take action and work on that one goal until it's complete. That will make you one of the highest-paid, most successful, and happiest people in your field.

Chapter Six

End Procrastination Now!

In this chapter, I'm going to cover the greatest enemy to productivity—the scourge of procrastination. It's the art of putting things off until someday on Someday Isle.

The number one reason for procrastination is that people have no sense of urgency about starting and completing a task. If you're walking across the street, and you hear a car honking and slamming on the brakes coming straight at you, you will move instantly. You won't have to sit down and wonder if this is a good use of your time or apply the 80/20 rule. You'll move instantaneously, because the urgency is so great.

People underachieve and fail because they don't have goals. They don't have goals written down, or organized, or broken down into plans with checklists. As a result, they engage in invisible procrastination. They're going to do it soon, later this morning, first thing this afternoon. "I'll do it before dinner; I'll catch up with it on the weekend."

Time drags out. It becomes habitual to delay the task until there is so much urgency that if you don't perform it, you're going to lose your job or your money. Then suddenly you're pushed into action, and what happens? You make mistakes. You make costly mistakes that if you had taken the time to think the task through, get organized, and do it on time, you would never have made. People are always saying, "Geez, if I'd just taken time to think about it, I wouldn't have done it that way."

Overcoming procrastination simply means doing things immediately until it becomes a habit. You want to develop the habit of planning your work, working your plan, and doing the most important things immediately.

One of the great questions that has shaped my life is, "What one great thing would you dare to dream if you knew you could not fail? If you were absolutely guaranteed success in anything, what goal would you set for yourself?"

In goal setting, I have people write down a list of ten goals, and then ask, "If I could have any one of these goals within twenty-four hours, which would have the greatest positive effect on my life?" Whatever it is, sort it out, and write it down, and make a list of the things that you could do to achieve the goal. Then organize the list by what you would do first, what you would do second, what you would third, and so on.

There's a famous story about Charles M. Schwab, one of the wealthiest men of the early twentieth century. (He was, by the way, not related to the Charles R. Schwab of investment fame.) He was president of Bethlehem Steel. In 1918 he wanted to make his executives more productive, so he brought in a famous consultant named Ivy Lee, who was one of the great pioneers of early public relations.

> **The number one reason for procrastination is because people have no *sense of urgency* about starting and completing a task.**

As the story goes, when Lee came in, Schwab asked him for a way to get more done.

"Give me fifteen minutes with your executives," said Lee.

"How much will it cost me?"

"Nothing. If you like what I've done, send me a check in three months to pay for what you think my advice is worth."

Ivy Lee gave the executives this advice.

1. At the end of each work day, write down the six most important things you need to accomplish tomorrow. Do not write down more than six tasks.
2. Prioritize those six items in order of their true importance.
3. When you arrive tomorrow, concentrate only on the first task. Work until the first task is finished before moving on to the second task.
4. Approach the rest of your list in the same fashion. At the end of the day, move any unfinished items to a new list of six tasks for the following day.
5. Repeat this process every working day.

Three months later, Schwab sent Ivy Lee a check for $25,000—the equivalent of $473,000 in 2019 dollars.

That's the most important way of dealing with procrastination: carefully think through and identify your most important task, the one task that can help you the most, the one activity that is setting the speed at which you are achieving your most important goal. Then discipline yourself to start on that, and work only on that until it's complete. If you can develop the discipline of making that your foremost work habit, you're going to be successful, and you'll probably be rich.

Implement the 5-steps for overcoming procrastination:

1. At the end of each work-day write down the six most important things you need to accomplish tomorrow. Do not write down more than six tasks.
2. Prioritize those six items in order of their true importance.
3. When you arrive tomorrow, concentrate only on the first task. Work until the first task is finished before moving on to the second task.
4. Approach the rest of your list in the same fashion. At the end of the day, move any unfinished items to a new list of six tasks for the following day.
5. Repeat this process every working day.

Affirmations

I've always been a huge proponent of affirmations. Your subconscious mind will accept anything that you say to yourself and believe. My early teacher in this area said, "With affirmations, statements that you make to yourself, your potential is unlimited." I never forgot those words.

The great tragedy is that 80 percent of people (here's the 80/20 rule again) talk to themselves in a negative way. They make statements such as, "I'm always late," or, "I never get everything done," or, "I wish I had more time." They sell themselves short, and use negative affirmations that sabotage their future.

I learned to say things to yourself that you want to be true. One of these is, "I always do it now. I always complete my tasks." If you make a mistake and fall back, and you don't get your task done, you say, "That's not like me. I always complete my tasks. Next time, I'll do it better. Next time, I'll finish it on time. Next time, I'll start earlier and stay at it until I complete it."

Always use those magic words, "Next time," because they cancel out the tendency to develop negative behavior habits. Always talk to yourself the way you want to be in the future. When you say things like, "I like myself; I can do it; I believe in myself; I'm the best," your subconscious mind accepts that as a command, and then organizes your thoughts, feelings, and behaviors to make them consistent with those words.

Start with the Hardest

Now I'm going to talk about the seven ways to overcome procrastination. The first one is to start your day with the most unpleasant task first. Earlier, I called it *Eat That Frog*. Eat the ugliest frog first. My friend Robert Allen says do the worst first. Do the one thing that you're more likely to procrastinate on than anything else and also the one thing that's going to make the most difference in your life if you start it and complete it.

What is it? Almost always it's a big task. It's an ugly task. It's a difficult task.

In America, about 65 percent of adults dream of starting a business someday, yet only one percent will ever do it. They can't get started, because they don't know how. We have thirty million businesses in America today. An enormous number were started by people who had never started a business before.

In other words, everyone has to learn, and starting a business is a very simple series of steps. I've written books on this subject. Years later, people have come back to me and said, "I found your book in the bookstore. I didn't try to be creative. I just did exactly what you said to do, step by step, chapter by chapter. Today I have a very successful business. I have more money than I ever dreamed I would ever have, and I'm rich. I'm happy. It just came from following the blueprint."

Another 84 percent of adults dream of writing a book someday. It's amazing. Recently I was driving with somebody and I said, "Do you know that 84 percent of adults think that they have a book inside them, yet only one percent will ever sit down and start to write a book?"

"I have a book in me," he said. "I want to write a book someday."

"Everybody wants to write a book someday. Why don't they? Because they don't get started."

When I wanted to write my first book, I went to a bookstore and bought a whole series of books about how to do it—how to organize your time, how to organize your subject, how to lay out the material. These books were all written by people who were professional writers, usually very successful ones. They had published many different books in other areas.

In America about 65% of adults dream of starting a business someday, yet only 1% will ever do it.

I put together a step-by-step checklist, and I began to write. When I finished my first book, which took an enormous amount of time, I wrote my second, and then my third. Then I found a most amazing thing about publishing and selling books: publishers will give you a little bit of promotional support for about ninety days; after that they go on to the next book.

Most publishers publish hundreds of books a year under many different imprints. After ninety days, nobody will help you. If you go to the radio stations or the bookstores, they'll say, "When did the book come out?"

"In April."

"We're sorry. This is August, and it's too late now." They won't interview you, they won't invite you to a book signing; they won't do anything.

So I said, "If a book is successful, it takes off in ninety days. If it's not successful, everybody just forgets about it. I'm going to spend $5,000 a month on a publicity agent to get interviews for me." Interviews are the only way you can get a book moving. Somebody has to say this is a good book. Somebody has to introduce it and tell people about it or interview you and have you tell people about it.

There's a whole art to doing a book interview. You can do an interview, and nothing will happen. You can do an interview, and the book will sell out in every bookstore in town within twenty-four hours. It all depends upon what you say. Most people have no idea what I'm talking about, because they never did their homework.

Anyway, I said, "I'm going to write a book every ninety days and work very hard to get that book moving, to help the book get legs. I'm going to work very hard, and if it doesn't work, I'm going to write a second book," so I began writing one book every ninety days.

People said, "That preposterous. You can't do that." But during the ninety days when I was promoting the most recent book, I was organizing myself, gathering my material, and following my process so I could write another book. Then I just did it; it was automatic.

Sometimes I have written and published five or six books in a year. These are not books that I published in my garage with a photocopier. They are published by the biggest publishers in the world. Can you do it? Yes, you can.

You learn, you organize your project in steps, and you do one step at a time. As you do, soon you will do more and more steps faster and faster, more and more easily; you become so productive that people say, "What are you smoking? What are you drinking? What do you eat? How is that you are so productive?"

The answer is, I think and decide on my most important task. Then I put my head down and work nonstop until that task is complete. If you do the same thing, you're going to get smarter, faster, and more competent. You'll also get happier and richer.

Negative Consequences

The second way to overcome procrastination is to think about the negative consequences of not completing the task.

Ask yourself: "If I don't do this task, what will happen?"

You have to use every mental trick possible to launch yourself into the task. That's the hardest thing of all for us, because we're so busy and preoccupied.

One way to launch yourself into the task is to think, "If I don't do this task, what will happen?"

When you take a university course, the first thing they tell you is that 50 percent of your grade will be your final paper. So do not wait. Do not put it off. Don't procrastinate. Start assembling your information and writing, because it has to be in on such and such a date in the professor's office, or you will fail.

People say, "Yes, yes, yes. We agree." But when are most term papers written? The night before. It's the coffeepot method of writing papers. I have had to write several papers on several subjects. What I did with every one of them is sit down at the kitchen table the night before the paper was due, clear everything off except what I needed to write it, put on a pot of coffee, and drink coffee all night. I would work all night to complete the paper, and then rush over to the university and push the paper under the professor's door so it could be there by 8:00 a.m. so I wouldn't fail the course.

In short, motivate yourself by thinking of the negative things that would happen if you didn't complete this task. How much would it cost you financially? How much would it cost you in promotion, in your career? Sometimes fear of that high cost will motivate you to complete the task.

Thinking about Benefits

The third way is the flip side: think about how you will benefit from doing the job or task. Look at it from the positive end. Say, "If I was really successful with this job, if I completed this task in such a way that it really worked, what would happen to me in my career? What would be the main benefit that I would enjoy?"

I have always lived like this. To go back to my example of working for the big boss, he said, "Here's a task I need you to do," I could say, what would be the downside if I didn't do this? I might lose my job. I might develop a reputation of being a person who doesn't do any work.

That's the downside. What's the upside? If I do this and do it well, I'm going to get more and more opportunities, I'm going to get them sooner, and I'm going to be paid more. So if it's going to help my career to do this job well, I'm going to add one more thing to it: to do it immediately. I'm going to do it faster. I'm going to say, "If my boss were asked what's the most important thing you want Brian to do in the near future, what would he say? Whatever it is, I'm going to do that, and do it immediately."

Set Aside Work Periods

The fourth idea is to set aside a designated fifteen-minute period during the day for working on your project.

Why did I select that particular amount of time? It's a short period. You can always find fifteen minutes, and it's easy to motivate yourself to get started. Once you get started, you work for fifteen minutes. You can have a timer, and the timer goes

---

Ask yourself: "If I was really successful with this job, what would be the main benefit that I would enjoy?"

---

off, bing, at the end of fifteen minutes, so you race against the time. You say, "How much can I get done in fifteen minutes? I've only got fifteen minutes, and then I can go back to the other things that I'm doing that are not as useful."

Very often, having done that work for fifteen minutes, you'll think, "Maybe I'll put in another fifteen minutes." Often you get pumped. You get excited. You want to. You can hardly wait, because you'll get this feeling of self-esteem and self-confidence. You get a feeling of happiness, of elation, when you start and complete part of a task.

If you keep doing that, pretty soon you will be your own motivator. You'll keep yourself pumped all the time.

Resist Perfectionism

The fifth way to overcome procrastination is to resist the tendency toward perfectionism.

Everybody has a little bit of a perfectionist tendency, but often people say, "If I can't do it perfectly because I don't have enough time, then I won't do it at all. I'll wait until I have enough time."

When writing books, I learned that it's not the writing that counts. It's the editing. Anybody can write, especially if you have a recording machine: you can record. You can write it, and that's what I started to do. I would dictate it with a professional recording machine, and then have a stenographer type it up.

Then I would take that, and I would go through it word by word and clean it up. Then I would do it again and clean it up. I found that the ideal for me was to write and rewrite a book five times. Don't even worry about the first time. The first time, just get it down on paper. This is the key to successful writing (often it's the key to completing any complex task). Then write it again and again and again.

I found the most amazing thing happens in book writing: when the book is finished, you will feel it. You will have a sense of relief and happiness. You can say to yourself, "It's done now. I can't make it any better than this," and then you can send it off.

I've had to do books as many as ten times because I simply couldn't get it to the point where I had that feeling that it was OK. I've found find that people who write music, design buildings, and do all sorts of creative things have that moment when they feel they can't do it better than this: "This is all I can do." Then they can stop. Then you take a deep breath, and you start your next project.

Nonetheless, there can be a temptation to keep putting a project off until you have every bit of knowledge you need. That day might never come if you hold that level of perfection.

Another use of the 80/20 rule: as long as you have your 80 percent of the knowledge and skills you need, get started. You'll get the extra 20 percent in learning along the way. This is a great idea. Resist the tendency towards perfectionism.

As long as you have 80 percent of the knowledge and skills you need, get started. You'll get the extra 20 percent in learning along the way.

Compulsion to Closure

A compulsion to closure means that you go to work on your own mind by saying, "I will work now. I will get this done now. I will complete this project this weekend, by 5:00 on Sunday, and I will not do anything else until I have finished it."

Then throw yourself into it. Keep saying, "I will work now. I will get this done now. I will complete this project immediately," and keep forcing yourself. "Do it now. Do it now. Do it now." Pump yourself up. Be your own cheerleader, and instead of thinking of reasons for not completing the task, think, "As soon as I complete this task, I'm going to go out to dinner, or I'm going to take a vacation." It's important to motivate yourself, because you're all you have.

In some companies, employees say that they have so many stillborn projects that they could have had a whole other level of profitability if they were to follow them through. They say, "Whatever happened to that project? It started, we planned it, we got it going, but somehow we drifted away."

Another factor is very important here: for a project to get done, there must be one person who is solely and exclusively responsible and rewarded for its successful completion.

In the Tom Peters book *In Search of Excellence: Lessons from America's Best-Run Companies*, we read that every successful company identified a champion, somebody who work single-mindedly for a single project. If they could not find a competent person who would take this task on, and devote themselves single-mindedly to completing it, they would not go ahead at all, because it would become an orphan. The orphan project would wander around the office. People would talk about it at meetings and say how it could be helpful, but nobody was responsible for it. Eventually the orphan would find an open door and disappear, and nobody would ever do it.

Earlier I mentioned ringing the glass—ding, ding, ding. Who's going to put the bell on the cat's tail? Who is going to be personally responsible for rewards and promotion on the successful completion of this task? If you don't have one person who will say, "It's me. I will accept full responsibility," then don't even attempt to make the task work by thinking that everybody else is going to do something miscellaneously.

One thing you can do to be successful in your career is always to raise your hand. Whenever a job needs to be done, raise your hand and say, "I'll do it." You only stop volunteering for more work when your boss says, "No. You already have enough on your plate. You are already busy enough. You have already volunteered to do too much."

The person who volunteers to do the things that need to be done for the success of the organization soon becomes the most admired and respected person in that company.

Because of the expediency factor, people seek the fastest and easiest way to get things done. Most people—the 80 percent who struggle for money all their lives—keep their hands down. They look away. They take a break and go to the bathroom. They say, "Don't look at me," because they're looking for ways to avoid work. You have to be the opposite: look for ways to do more work.

Remember, the time is going to pass anyway. The days, the weeks, the months are going to pass. The only question is, where will you be at the end of this time? Will you be back in

---

Whenever a job needs to be done, raise your hand and say "I'll do it."

---

the same place, doing the same low level of work, or will you be moving ahead faster and faster?

The time is going to pass anyway. At the end of your working life, you can be rich, or you can be poor, and it's very much your decision. It's not decided by your boss or the economy or the politicians or the competition. *You* decide how much you earn over the course of your life. If you're not happy with your current income, go to the nearest mirror and negotiate with your boss, and say, "Boss, I want more money."

Your boss will say, "You'd better get out there and get some more responsibility. Get out there and get that arm loosened up, and raise your hand. Offer to do things." Simultaneously, use evenings and weekends to upgrade your skills, so you can do the things that you have volunteered to do at a higher and better level.

A young woman came to work for me when I started my business, and she'd just been fired from a loan and trust company. They didn't like her, but she was young. She was twenty-one when she came to work for me, and her self-esteem was quite low. I was able to get her at $1,200 a month, which was great. She was the all-purpose secretary.

Work went on, the job went on. The company started to become more successful. I noticed that the secretary started to become more productive. She came to me after a month and said, "You know, we don't have anybody keeping the books."

"No," I said, "I haven't really thought about that."

"Look, I'll take care of the books and the finances, and I'll pay the bills if that's OK with you."

"Sure," I said.

Later that she had taken a course in accounting at a community college, and she had set up all of our books. So that was off my shoulders. Then she had a new computer and new programs installed so she could type and process more letters, put out more communication, and create advertisements, and she went back to work.

She'd been working for me for six months. One day she came to me. I'd been paying her $1,200 a month, and she said, "I'd like to talk to you about earning more money."

"Absolutely," I said. "You're doing a great job. I was thinking of giving you an extra $100 a month. How about that?"

"Well, thank you very much," she said. "It's a nice thought, but I have been looking in the marketplace for people with the skills to do the things that I do in a company, and I think that my job is worth closer to $2,000 a month. I would like you to think about that in terms of increasing my pay."

I almost had a heart attack. She was working for $1,200 a month, and now she wanted $2,000 a month, but I realized she was right. She had made herself indispensable. She was doing the work of two or three people. As my company was growing, she was growing.

So, clever person that I am, I negotiated her down to $1,800 a month. I gave her an increase from $1,200 to $1,800 a month. That's a $600 increase—a 50 percent increase in six months. She said, "Thank you very much," she said, and she went back to work.

"Thank God I got away with $1,800 a month," I said. This little girl, twenty-one years old, had negotiated me into a 50 percent raise in six months simply by becoming better and better at doing more and more of the things that I needed doing.

She said another thing: "If you tried to hire someone else with my skills, you'd have to pay them more than $2,000 a month, because the skills that I have are irreplaceable, and you cannot grow your company without my skills."

I realized she was right. She was prepared. She was organized. She'd upgraded her skills, and she worked with me for a long time. I increased her pay up to $3,000 and $4,000 a month. By the age of twenty-five, she was earning more than her parents had earned at the age of forty-five and fifty-five. Finally she left because she and her husband moved to a different city.

Think about that. Keep looking for ways. How can I make myself more valuable? Then do it now. Do it immediately. Get on with it.

Keep a Fast Tempo

The seventh idea for overcoming procrastination is to maintain a fast tempo. I've already talked about that sense of urgency, but this has to do with keeping your pace at a certain consistent level.

We are all creatures of habit. It's very easy to become comfortable with a slow-paced level of work. However, successful people move quickly. They have an idea, they make a call. They have an idea, they immediately go online.

Today any new information you need is available on the iPhone in a couple of seconds. You can go to a movie, and you can learn everything about it—the story, the actors, the writers, the past, the future, the money. It's astonishing how much you can learn, and how quickly you can learn it. Then you can take action. You can move quickly.

Fast tempo means when you go to work, get on with it. Take two stairs at a time when you climb the stairs. When you walk, walk faster. When you get to work, get to work immediately, and work quickly. Work all the time you work.

You can do twice as much in a day without strain really by just working quickly and getting at it. Don't take two hours for lunch. Take twenty minutes, and then get back to work. Keep saying these words, "Back to work. Back to work."

Move faster, move smarter, and learn new skills that enable you to get more done in that same period of time.

The 7 Ways to overcome procrastination:

1. Start your day with the most unpleasant task first. Eat that frog!
2. Think about the negative consequences of not completing the task.
3. Think about how you will benefit from doing the job or the task.
4. Set aside a designated fifteen-minute period during the day for working on your project.
5. Resist the tendency toward perfectionism.
6. Develop a "compulsion to closure" of your task or project.
7. Maintain a fast tempo.

Live Consciously

I do believe in one type of procrastination. It's called *creative procrastination*.

For many years, a gentleman named Nathaniel Branden, one of the great American thinkers and philosophers of the last century, was a friend of mine. I read many of his books. He wrote on many things, including self-esteem. For him, self-esteem was the critical factor in human relationships. He was once asked, "If you could give one piece of advice to people after an entire lifetime of thinking about this, what would it be?"

"To live consciously," he said. "Live consciously." Most people live unconsciously. They respond and think and go through their lives automatically. They'll drive from home to work without remembering a single second of the trip, because their minds were off and drifting.

Procrastination is living unconsciously. You're not even aware of it. Nobody says, "OK, I'm going to procrastinate now for a certain period of time on these specific tasks." We do it automatically.

Living creatively, procrastinating creatively, on the other hand, means that you deliberately think through the things that you are going to do. You don't let them happen accidentally, because the accidental things are often the factors that can change your whole life.

You think it through, and you creatively decide that this particular activity is something that I am not going to do now. I may or may not do it at a later time, but I am not going to do this now. This is not a good use of my time. This is not the most valuable use of my time. It's a good idea, but not at this time.

***Creative procrastination* means that you deliberately think through the things that you are going to do.**

You're very clear and deliberate about it: consciously, I am not going to do this activity, because it's not a good use of my time, and it takes me away from doing the things that can make a real difference in my life and work.

If you do not consciously and creatively procrastinate, which means deliberately deciding on those things that you are *not* going to do at this moment, you will automatically and unthinkingly procrastinate on the most important things that you could be doing.

Be very clear and conscious. Your job is to be the most successful person you can possibly be. This means starting and completing your most important tasks and spending no time at all on those tasks that do not contribute to the things that you want to accomplish.

Chapter Seven

Productivity Tips to Fast-Track Your Career

In business, I help companies develop strategic plans. The biggest company I've ever worked for had $140 billion and 22,000 employees. I was able to help them reorganize the entire company, so it was vastly more profitable and growing far faster.

One question we ask is, "Who is my customer?" If you say, "The person who buys my product or service," no. It's actually something bigger than that. Your customer is anyone who depends on you for anything that you do at work. Of course, it's true at home. Your family is your customer as well, because they depend upon you and the things you do.

Your Most Important Customer

Your boss is also your customer. Customer satisfaction is boss satisfaction, and it's one of the most important things that you do. Actually, your boss is your most important customer.

I've already discussed making lists. Here is another version. Make a list of everything that you think you are hired to do. Take it to your boss, and ask your boss to organize the items by order of priority. "If I could only do one thing on this list, which would it be? Which do you think is the most important thing that I do? Which is number two; which is number three?"

The most important thing you can do at work is to be working on your boss's list of priorities. Nothing will make your boss happier, nothing will get you paid more and promoted faster, than to be always working on what they consider to be more important than anything else. With changes in the economy, the competition, and the market, these priorities can change very quickly. Your boss can give you an answer on Monday, and what they need you to do quickly and well on Tuesday may be different.

Keep in regular touch with your boss. Instead of having conversations that may go round and round, say, "Here's my list. Please organize my list by priority. If I can only do three things today, what are the three things that you would want me to do and get back to you?"

Keep coming back to this. When your boss knows you are working on what is most important to him or her, your boss is going to be happy and is going to give you more and more help. Your boss is going to help you to get more training so you can do more of these things.

The person who buys your product or service in the marketplace is, of course, very important as a customer, because their satisfaction determines the future of your company, and your contribution to that satisfaction determines *your* future. So it's really important to keep thinking about the future, the biggest

---

**The most important thing you can do at work is
to be working on your boss's list of priorities.**

---

single contribution you can make, and whom you can make this contribution to.

Hierarchy

Should people waste much time worrying about whether their results are visible to their boss? We do see a lot of office politics behavior, when people who will only do something that their boss can see. If it has to do with helping their coworkers, they don't think the boss sees that. They might ignore it, so you have sometimes these situations where someone is popular with the boss, but the rest of the coworkers don't like them or don't feel they're helpful.

Should you worry about office politics, or should you just focus adding value without worrying whether it's visible?

A great philosopher said that the first law of human activity is hierarchy. It's the order of people in their society and their business and their club. The Catholic church has eight levels of hierarchy. There is the pope at the top, and then there are cardinals and archbishops, and so on, down to the parish level.

Everyone who works within this hierarchy knows where they are, who is above them, and who is below them. Everyone is ambitious to the degree to which they want to move up in the hierarchy. They want to go higher and higher, because the higher they go, the more rewards they receive, the more respect and the more money they have. So you have to ask yourself where you are in the hierarchy and what your goal is.

Now the role of a company, a private business, is to produce a product or service that enriches the life or work of a customer, and to do it better than your competitors. Then you sell as much of it as you possibly can and make a profit. As we've seen, profits are the cost of tomorrow. Where there is no profit, there is no tomorrow.

How does a person move up to become your boss? They become better than other people at achieving those goals, at producing the product or service, at selling and marketing it in a competitive market, and bringing in the hay—bringing home rewards.

Your job is to please your boss. Once at a seminar a woman came up to me and said, "I want to take exception to what you said. My job is not to please my boss. My job is to do my work and get along with my coworkers, but it's not to please my boss. If my boss wants me to please him, that's his problem."

"What a tragedy," I said. "Your job is not to please your boss? Then why are you working? Why have you been hired? Why have you been given this responsibility? In hierarchies, people hire people under them in order to help them do their jobs. Your job is to help the people above you to do their job."

My focus has always been on serving my boss. If my boss needs this and needs this now, or wants this and wants it tomorrow, that's my job. If I can do that well, I'm going to be guaranteed a great job and high pay and promotion. So remember: your job is to please your boss.

People say, "My job is to get along with my coworkers." No, it's not, unless getting along with your coworkers is essential to

---

**Ask yourself: "Where am I in the hierarchy of
my company, and what is my goal?"**

---

doing your job and taking care of your boss's most important
needs. Be clear about what you're doing. There's a lot of claptrap
by people who've never worked in a company. They say your job
is to get along with your coworkers and to be happy at work, and
to think about your own happiness before anything else.

No, it's not. Your job is to make a contribution that is much
greater in value than the amount that it costs to keep you on
the payroll. Wonderfully enough, you are your own boss, and
if you want to talk to your boss, go to the nearest mirror, and
discuss your job with your boss. That person will tell you what
you need to do. As for the person who hires you, your job is to
think only, "I want to make a great contribution."

When working with my boss, I've always been very clear.
"What can I do to help you to do your job better? What's the
most important thing I can do? Here are the things that I am
working on." Clarity, clarity, clarity.

In many cases, people think, "My job isn't to please my
boss. My job is just to do my job." They do their job, and they
do it well, but the boss isn't even aware of it, because they think,
"I don't have to tell my boss. It's my boss's job to figure this out
for himself or herself."

No, it's not. Your job is to do the job well, *and* to show the
boss you've done it well and what a difference it makes.

This is not playing politics. It's being absolutely clear about
what is most important to your boss. It's about not getting off
on the wrong track and starting to work on something that is of

no importance to your boss at all. In fact, more than one great management consultant has said that the worst use of time is to do very well what need not be done at all. It's called *the law of the excluded alternative.* The very worst use of time is to work hard to do something well that need not be done at all, or at least need not be done now.

Be sure that what you are working on needs to be done now, and that it's important to your boss. Your job is to make your boss happy, because that's how you get promoted faster and paid more. Your boss will notice your performance and realize, "I don't want this person to leave. This person is valuable to me. Anything I ask them to do, they do it quickly. They do more work than two or three other people."

Remember, in every company, 80/20 applies; 20 percent of the staff do 80 percent of the work, and 20 percent of the staff make all the money. The 20 percent of the staff are given the tickets to the Bahamas for the weekend with their spouse. The 20 percent of the staff are the ones who are continually paid more and given cars and bigger offices and staff. That's the person that you want to be, and you do not become this person accidentally. You become this person deliberately by focusing on it: "I want to become more. I'm going to become more and more valuable every single day."

Face Time and Effort

Companies often put a lot of focus on visibility—being seen at work early and late and visibly making efforts. Is this important, or is it all about results? How important is face time with a boss?

The Law of the Excluded Alternative says that the worst use of time is to do very well what need not be done at all.

I have seen many situations where the boss evaluates the staff based on the number of hours that they put in. He comes to work and does a head check. How many people are here? Maybe work starts at 8:00, and so he'll go in at 7:00 and look around to see how many came in early. He'll wait until the end of the day to see how many people left.

I've seen companies where everybody stays until the boss goes home. They may not be doing anything. They may be hanging out. They may be fooling around on their email. They may be chatting with each other, but they all just bide their time until the boss leaves.

Napoleon Hill told wonderful story about a young man who got a job with a big company. He really wanted to be successful. He was in an office with a large open pit with a lot of desks. He had one desk in this grouping.

The young man noticed that his boss always came into work at about 7:30 and left at about 6:00 or 6:30. The young man would always come to work at 7:00. When his boss arrived, he was always there and working, and he would always go home at 6:30, so when his boss left, he was still there working. He was the first one in and the last one out every day.

One day, the boss, who had ignored him for quite a while, came up to him and said, "I see that you're always here when I arrive in the morning, and you're always here when I leave. What is this all about? Why are you doing this?"

"I just wanted to be sure that I'm available if you have something that you need me to do."

"Oh," said the boss, "that's an interesting philosophy. Thank you," and he went home.

A few days later, the boss called him in at 6:00, and said, "I'd like you to do this for me. It's kind of important. It just came up a few minutes ago. Can you fit this into your schedule?"

"Absolutely," said the young man. He took the project and went to work on it. He got it all done the next day and handed it in.

"Thank you very much," said the boss. "I appreciate that." The boss critiqued the young man's work, saying he could improve it here and there.

A couple of days went by. The boss called young man in again in the middle of the day and said, "Something has come up. Could you take care of this for me?"

Soon the boss was talking to him every day; soon, two or three times a day. Soon the young man was working nonstop on the boss's top projects. He was promoted and moved to a bigger desk closer to the head office. Soon he had his own office. By the time he was thirty-five, he was the vice president of an international company. He was liked and respected and admired by everybody he worked for, because from the beginning of his career, his focus was on helping his boss, whoever the boss was.

Don't ever let anybody talk you into the idea that you're not here to please or help your boss. That's the only reason that you're at your job. If you don't like the fact that your boss wants you to do or not do certain things, change jobs.

**Don't ever let anybody talk you into the idea that
you are not here to please or help your boss.**

Volunteer for work for your boss, and when you're caught up, go and say, "I'm caught up with all my work. I want more work."

I like to work. If you don't, you really have to give a lot of thought to what you're doing, because the great majority of people don't like to work, and they look for every way to avoid working. They keep their heads down so their boss doesn't choose them for a job.

When I went to my boss and said, "I want more work," he would ignore me. I even reached the point where I had all my work done and I was thinking of quitting, because I wanted more work. Finally the dam broke, and he started to give me job after job, like dealing cards one card at a time.

After that, my working life was wonderful. I was running three divisions of the company and generating millions of dollars of sales and revenue. I was hired away and moved up, and I'd began to teach what I had learned to executives of other companies. They hired me to work in their companies and brought me in to teach strategic planning.

Be sure that you love your work. Remember that, as Napoleon Hill pointed out, if you love your work, you'll never work another day in your life. Your job at the beginning of your career is to find work that you love to do. Find work that you're eager to do, so staying after to do more work is a joy. You can hardly wait. Then you have to work to balance this with your family and relationships.

I have many friends who are at the top of their field, and they love to work. They're in early, they work hard, they love to work on the weekends, and they're also the highest-paid people in our society. They make enormous amounts of money, but they love the work. We joke that we have to discipline ourselves *not* to work. We like working so much that we have to hold ourselves back. It's a joy.

If you get to the point where your work is a joy, you're going to have an incredible life. You're going to be happy all the time, and you're going to be one of the highest-paid people in your field. You're going to grow and grow. You'll always be looking for ways to do your work better and to do more of it.

When I began to move up in different organizations and industries—surprise, surprise, the law of attraction—I began to be attracted to, and attracted to me, the top people in that field, first locally, and then statewide, and then nationally, and then internationally. I have friends all over the world that have gone out of their way to meet me personally because they had heard about the good work that I did in their field. Everybody wants to know the people who do good work in the field they love.

Here's another thing. All the best people that I have met, at the end of our first conversation, say to me, "Is there anything that I can do for you? Is there anything that I can help you with?"

I hear this at least once a week from people who contact me and say, "How can I help you? Is there any way that I can help you?" They don't know much about my personal life or business, but they are eager to help people who are going somewhere with their lives.

**"Is there anything else I can do for you?
Is there anything that I can help you with?"**

In addition, you should always look for ways to do more than you're paid for. Look for ways to put in more than you take out. Look for ways to help people to be more successful. I've done this for decades, and it has come back to pay off five and ten and fifty and 100 times.

Recently I was at a seminar in Dallas. Another speaker, who's known all over the country, came up and said, "Before I start, I want to point out this man because he has had such a profound influence on my life," and he pointed to me. He said, "He taught me one thing that I had never heard before, and it changed my life forever. He said read two to three hours a day. Continually upgrade your skills. Get better and better at what you do. I was working hard, but the importance of upgrading my skills had never dawned on me. So I read two to three hours every day in my field.

"I heard him say this at a big seminar when I was eighteen years old. My biggest goal at that time was to become a millionaire. I came from an Army family. My mother has gone away. My father was an Army sergeant and was pretty tough on me. I went to an average school, and I got average grades. Somebody bought me a ticket and took me to this seminar."

In that seminar, I said, work, learn, study, raise your skills. "By the time I was twenty-five," he said, "I was a millionaire. By the time I was thirty, I was a double and triple millionaire. I'm thirty-five today, and I now have more money than I can spend for the rest of my life. It's all because of what he said to me at that time."

Telecommuting and Self-Discipline

Let me talk about a topic that's very germane to the economy we live in today: telecommuting, or working from home.

Can working from home can be a productive option? If someone's given the choice to work at the company or to work from home, which is more productive for people who want to move up in their work lives?

To answer this, we come back to our friend discipline. As Napoleon Hill said, "Discipline is the master key to riches." With it, all things are possible, and without it, nothing is possible.

What is the problem with working from home? It's lack of discipline. People don't work at home. Every so often, they do a little bit of work. Then they may have something to eat and watch a little TV, maybe read the paper, and so on.

Personally, I now do a lot of work at home. I have written more than eighty books at home at the same desk, with the same computer and the same printing equipment. I sit down, I get organized, and I start to write. I'm very capable of working by myself.

I have two or three people on staff, and they work out of their own homes. Everyone is extremely well-disciplined. They do wonderful work, and they do it quickly, even if they're overseas. They keep in touch by computer, and they keep on top of things so they are always on time. They always do good work. These people can work at home all day long, because

What's the main problem with working from home? It's lack of discipline.

they're well-disciplined, they're well-organized, and they get a lot done.

We work in offices because for decades, maybe even a couple of centuries, every worker depended upon the others. Each person did a little of a task, and they passed it on to the next person, and so on. More and more time was spent in meetings dividing up the task, discussing it, taking it apart, and so on. Today, with computers, we can have face-to-face contact through Skype or Zoom or similar modes. We can talk to one person or a group of people.

I now do coaching seminars for between 150 and 200 people worldwide. I do them four times a month for one hour, and I do them on Zoom. People enroll in the coaching program. We send them information on what we'll be talking about, and then we send them assignments, and then we make ourselves available for questions that they have. We send them books and CDs to listen to.

Two to four times a month, I meet with hundreds of people all over the world, and we talk face-to-face. I ask and answer questions. We do not need to be in the same room together. We can be on the same screen together.

With the technology of Zoom, which is now booming as a high-tech startup, you can see the pictures of everybody else who is on the call with you. You can talk to them; you can call one another out, and ask and answer questions. It's like being in a big room with people.

The only time you need to go into an office is when face-to-face interaction is essential to doing the job correctly and well. This is especially true for a new job, a new company, a new business, new technology, new sales and marketing—situations where you're learning a lot at a rapid rate. Then it's very important that you get head-to-head with people and share your experiences. If you don't, it can take you five or ten or twenty times as long to get up to the same level of skill and results.

Always ask, "Can I do all of these things at home, or do I need to be in the same room with people talking?" My best friends in the company do both. They work long hours at home, and they go into the office for long hours. They make sure that every minute counts.

Plan every meeting so that you have your meeting at 11:00, and everyone is sitting there ready to go at three minutes to 11:00. The meeting is over at 11:55. Then you have your next meeting or lunch. It's a matter of planning and preparation.

Teamwork

Tom Peters once said, "All work is done by teams." Early in your career, your ability to work on a team and to be a major contributor to the team, starts you up the fast track to success. Later, your ability to assemble and lead a team will largely determine your success in life.

Many years ago, I had a great opportunity to work with a Fortune 500 company that had one of the best reputations in the world for the motivation, self-esteem, and esprit de corps of their people. People would crawl over broken glass to work for this company. They had one of the best training programs in the world.

They asked me if I would do a leadership seminar for them. The man who hired me said, "Before you give this leadership talk, which is on additional subjects to what we teach, I would like you to read our leadership guide."

They had hired one of the biggest management consulting companies in the world. Over two or three years, they had done a study of 120 teams in this company that had pulled off extraordinary achievements of productivity. These teams had reduced the manufacturing costs of a competitive product by 80 percent, started and built a division for a new product, and became the world leader within six months. The company brought the consultants in. They identified five qualities that the top teams had.

The man said, "I want to give you my manual. The manual is numbered, it is signed out, and it is confidential. Before you talk to our leaders, I want you to read this through so you know what we have taught these people, and what they work on every day. However, you are not allowed to copy it, and you're not allowed to take notes from it. You're only allowed to read it so that you understand it, and give it back to me on Monday morning."

This was on Thursday or Friday, so I started to page through it. I said, "Oh, my God. Jeez, this is good stuff!" All day Saturday and Sunday, I read and reread this material, walked around, and remembered as much as I could.

So from my experience and millions of dollars of research, here are the five key principles of the most successful teams. These are the keys to great success.

1. **Clear goals and objectives.** The team would sit down and talk for however many hours it took to be crystal clear about what they were trying to accomplish—dramatic improvements in quality, dramatic reductions in cost, expansion of markets, market growth—until everybody was clear about the goals and agreed on them.

2. **Clear values.** The teams discussed the values they would use to guide their behavior toward one another: punctuality, friendliness, cooperation, helpfulness, doing one's share of the work, upgrading one's skills.

3. **Clear plans of action.** The team would ask, "What are we going to do to achieve the goal? What is each person going to do to achieve the goal? What contribution will they be expected to make?" Everyone knew what every other person on the team was contributing. When they had meetings to discuss the work, everyone knew what everyone else was supposed to have done since the last meeting.

4. **Lead the action.** This was really aimed at the leader or the manager. It said that you lead people by inspiration. You don't tell them what to do; you get them to agree about what you want to accomplish together: this is the goal; these are the values you stand by; this is what everybody is going to contribute. The leader's primary job is to make sure that each person has everything they need to make their contribution: they have the right equipment, the right amount of time, the right assistance or personnel.

5. **Continual review and evaluation.** Next, you look at how you're doing on a regular basis "How are we doing? Are

we doing a good job? Are we making progress? Are we achieving our goals? Is everybody making their expected contribution?"

I've taught those five principles to hundreds of thousands of managers. People come back and say it's transformed their businesses.

Unless everybody is perfectly clear about all of these things, people will start to work, often very hard, on things that are of low value. They won't fulfill their contribution to the team. They won't get the job done on time. When they come to the meetings, they won't be punctual.

So the teams constantly discuss clear goals, clear values, and clear plans of action. Then they lead the action and constantly review and make sure that they are getting better and better at what they do.

Five Key Principles of the Most Successful Teams:

1. Clear Goals and Objectives.
2. Clear Values.
3. Clear Plans of Action.
4. Lead the Action.
5. Continual Review and Evaluation.

Doubling Your Sales

Sales is a profession where productivity is particularly important. Here productivity is the basis of how your results are measured, how many sales you make, and how satisfied your customers are. It also determines how much you are paid and how far you advance in the organization.

There's been research into selling and the time management of salespeople that goes back to 1927—how much salespeople earn, how much the highest salespeople earn, and the transition point from low sales and income to high sales.

The results turn out to be very much the same. The average salesperson works only about 20 or 30 percent of the time. The rest of the time they spend warming up, warming down, coming in late and leaving early, and going out for lunch with their friends. Today they spend a lot of time on the computer and online, but still they only spend about two hours a day working. In an eight-hour day, six hours is somehow spent going from place to place, and it's wasted.

What determines your income if you're in sales? It is the number of minutes that you spend face-to-face with people who can and will buy your product or service within a reasonable period of time. So if you want to double your income, it's very simple. Calculate that today you're spending two hours face-to-face with customers. (That's the average; some are above, and some are below.) Decide to increase the time you spend with customers over the next month to four hours per day. That still leaves you four hours to goof off, check your email, and take long lunches.

If you are earning a given amount of money by seeing customers two hours a day, by the law of probabilities, you'll double your income by seeing customers twice as much. You may not know where the sale is going to come from or which customer is going to buy, but if you double your face time, you double your income.

In order to double your income in sales, decide to increase the time you spend with customers over the next month to *four hours* per day.

The next thing is to get better and better at your most important tasks. When you double your face time, you also double your skill level. Then you triple your face time.

If you want to be one of the highest-paid people in the sales world, you have to organize your life so that you spend 80 percent of your time face-to-face with customers who can and will buy from you. This is the greatest time management technique of all. Master your key skills, and spend more and more time practicing those skills face-to-face with your customers.

As for measuring your results, in sales the only measure is the amount of money that you earn—the amount of sales that you generate for your company and the amount of it that you keep in commissions, salaries, and bonuses.

I always start off a sales seminar by saying, "Before we start, let me ask a question. Why do you get up in the morning?" Everybody stops, and I say, "You get up in the morning to make more money. You go to work to make more money. You don't want to make less money, and you don't want to make the same amount of money. You want to make more money. Would you agree with that?"

They all nod their heads. I say, "So how do you make more money?" I call it MMM. "How do you MMM, *make more money*? You *sell more stuff*. That's how you make more money. Your job is to MMM by SMSing. How do you sell more stuff? You get face-to-face with people who can buy your product within a reasonable period of time. This means that if you are not face-to-face with a customer, you are not working. You are actually unemployed. You are a useless member of society. In fact, if you're not face-to-face with customers, you should go home, go back to bed, and pull up the covers over your head, because you're of no value to your family or to everyone else. Wouldn't you agree?"

Everybody says, "Oh!" but they realize it's true. If you are not getting face-to-face with people and asking them to buy your product, you're not working. You're basically wasting your time, and you're wasting the time of the people in your company.

Some years ago, I worked with a sales manager. He's one of the best in the country. He took over one of the worst-performing bureaus of one of the biggest multinational companies in the country.

The first thing the new manager did was to say at the morning meeting, "Let me ask you a question before we begin. What is it that you do *not* see in this office?" They looked around to see if he had taken some pictures off the wall or something, and finally they gave up.

"There are no customers in this office," said the manager. "Your job is to meet face-to-face with customers and to sell them our product. Therefore you have to get out of here and get to work talking to people."

Surprise, surprise—there are no customers inside your company. There's nobody in your company that can buy any of your products. Therefore if you're in the office, there's nobody there who can help you MMM or SMS. You have to get out of the office.

The salespeople had been used to coming in, shooting the breeze, and drinking coffee until 10:30 or 11:00, and then strolling out to make a call or two, and then going for lunch. At 8:35, the sales meeting was over. So they all went out and said, "Who does this character think he is?" They used a few swear words.

"Does anybody want to go out for a cup of coffee?"

"Yes, I'll go with you. We'll go down the street to Starbucks," and they walked out. A couple of them said, "Well, I might as well go and call on a couple of customers," because this company did good advertising and had a good reputation and had good leads.

Some of them went out and called on customers, and, surprise, surprise, by the law of probabilities, they made a couple of sales. The next day, they walked into the office, and all of the furniture was gone. There were two or three closing offices with desks and chairs, but the rest of the furniture was gone.

The manager said, "Now what do you notice is missing in this office?"

They said, "All the furniture is gone. There's no place to sit."

"Yes, you're correct," he said. "We had a furniture company come in yesterday while you were all out seeing customers, and we had them take all the furniture away. We won't need the furniture in this office, because you're not going to be spending any time in this office. If you do bring back a customer, there are three offices here where you can go privately and talk to them, but other than that, we won't need any furniture at all."

Again, they were furious. This was not the way they were accustomed to work with the previous bosses (each one of which had been fired for poor performance).

"All right," said the manager. "Now we're going to have sales meetings every morning for fifteen minutes. We're going to talk about sales principles, and they're going to be stand-up meetings, so you're not going to have to sit down and take notes. For fifteen minutes every morning, we're going to talk about how we can make more sales."

The manager began to train them. They'd already been trained very well, but he began to reinforce the training. He began to ask people, "Where are we weak? What do we need to do more of in today's market?"

The salespeople would say, "We need some help on closing," or, "We need some help on overcoming objections."

"Great. We'll talk about that tomorrow."

The next day the manager would say, "All right. Let's talk about handling objections. What are the biggest objections that cause people to hold back from buying our product?"

"Well, we get this, and we get that."

"Does anybody here have any answers? How do you answer that?"

One said, "Whenever I hear that objection, I say this."

Someone else said, "Whenever I hear that, I say this."

Another one said, "That's a great idea," and they started to take notes.

Then the manager said, "OK, it's 8:45. Let's go to work."

Out of 2,000 sales offices, this one started off at number 2,000. It was number 1,000 at the end of one year, and at the end of two years, it was the number one organization in the world for this company. The manager became a legend in high-tech sales, because he got everybody out there talking to customers.

If you are your own boss, you have to practice these principles yourself. There are no customers in your office. If you are in your office, that means you are unofficially unemployed. You are not working. You're a waste of time for yourself and your company, so get out there and see people.

As a salesperson, if you are sitting in your office, you are officially unemployed. You are not working.

Sales: The Seven-Part Recipe

Now let's talk about the seven key parts of the sales process: the recipe for selling.

1. **Prospecting.** You have to find people who can be helped by your product or service. The more people you talk to, by the law of probabilities, the more likely it is that one of those people will buy your product.

2. **Building rapport and trust with the person you're talking to.** All sales are made on the basis of emotion. It means that people like you and trust you. As a result, they like and trust what you say about your product or service, and they're willing to buy and use it.

   So you have to take the time to slow down, gear back, and make a friend of your prospects. Ask them questions about themselves, their life, their work, what they're doing now, and how it's working. In every relationship where you're talking to another person, when that person likes you and is going to become a friend, you will feel a click. Something will happen, and the person will smile, lean forward, and say, "Well, what do you have?"

It's clear: "I like you, I trust you, and I'm interested in your product."

You say, "Well, let me ask you a couple of questions first." Then you ask questions to find out exactly what the prospect is doing now in the area of your product and how it is working for them. You ask what their goals are, what they want to accomplish, what kind of a budget they have, what they've done in the past, and where they hope to be in the future, so that you really understand.

3. **The diagnostic phase.** It's like a doctor working with a patient. If you go to any doctor in the world, the first thing they'll do is as thorough a diagnosis as they possibly can. You would never expect a doctor to recommend a course of treatment before they diagnosed you thoroughly. Sometimes they'll take tests. The tests will go out, and you'll have to go back and see the doctor once he gets the results.

So take your time. See yourself as a doctor of selling, and the first part of being a doctor is asking questions. You diagnose the customer's situation.

4. **The presentation.** Here you present your product based on what you've discussed up to now. You explain, "Based on what you said you wanted and needed, this is what the product will do for you."

We find that when we repeat what the customer said back to them, they won't argue. The first rule of communication is that no one argues with their own data; no one argues with what they themselves have said. If they said this is what they wanted and needed, and you say, "You said this is what you wanted and needed, and this is what the product will do," they're not going to argue with you. They're going to nod like a little toy dog in the back of a pickup truck. They're going to be nodding and nodding as you make your presentation based on what they told you they needed and wanted.

5. **Answering objections.** Every customer has objections. Every customer wants to reduce the risk of making a wrong decision, so they will ask you questions. "What about this, what about that?" Your job is to be thoroughly prepared so that when they give you an objection, you are prepared for it, and you can say, "That is a good question."

Always respond to an objection by saying, "That is a good question. Let me see if I can answer it for you." Then you answer and show that it is not a reason for not buying your product or service. Then you say, "Anything else? Any other concerns that you may have?"

You do not close the sale until the customer says, "No, it sounds pretty good to me." If you try to close the sale before you reach the point where the customer is ready to buy, you'll kill the sale. You'll be thanked for your time, you'll be ushered to the door, and you'll never see that person again. The timing is really important.

6. **Close the sale.** How do you close the sale? You ask the customer to make a buying decision.

I've found that you need only a few ways to ask for the order. Different products and services are sold in different ways, but one of the best ways of closing the sale is to say, "Well, if you have no further questions, then the next step is this." Then you explain the plan of action and what you'll do now. "I'll need your signature on this application form. I'll need a check from you for his amount. We'll get it back to the office. It'll be out for you on Tuesday, and we'll have an installer on Wednesday who will show you how to use it about 10:00 in the morning. Is that OK?"

In other words, explain the process to them; we call it *talking past the sale*. We say, "If you have no further questions, this is the next step for you to buy the product. Here's how you buy it. Here's what you do. Here's when we will install it, and here's the next step." Then you say to the customer, "How does that sound?" The customer says, "Sounds great."

7. **Get resales and referrals.** Resales are where you sell the customer your product again and again. Most of the successful companies in the world are based on repeat sales. The customers are so happy that they buy again and again, and they tell their friends.

The second part is referrals. The easiest person to sell to is a good referral. Someone they like and respect has bought your product and has recommended it to them.

Always keep going back and making sure that your customer is happy. Then ask your customer for the names of other people who might be interested in your product as well.

When I started off, I had no idea that sales was a learnable skill. My first problem was establishing rapport and trust. I had to get people to like me, because people were saying very early in the conversation, "Thanks for coming in, but I'm really not interested," or "This is not a good use of your time," or "We're really busy today."

When I started asking questions, listening to the answers, and asking follow-up questions, customers became interested in knowing what I was selling and how it might benefit them. Once I mastered that—which was quite simple, by the way; you can do it almost in one sales lesson—the biggest problem for me was closing the sale, getting them to take action now rather than delaying to a later time.

So I began to do a full-court press on closing the sale. I got every book and audio program I could find. I read them and listened to them over and over every day. I walked around with the audio programs in my ear. At breaks in the morning, and in the evening, and whenever I had time off, I read the books and underlined them. I practiced like an actor practicing for a play in front of a mirror until I could close sales like nothing you could believe.

My sales in the next twelve months went up ten times. I became the top salesperson in the international organization, and I made more money with more people working for me on overrides and commissions than I ever dreamed possible.

Wonderful news: every person—shy people, educated people, uneducated people—have the ability to become absolutely excellent in selling. It's an eminently learnable skill, and 17 percent of people in our society work in sales. Their income is directly dependent on their ability to make a sale, get the money, and take it home or back to the office.

If 17 percent of people can make that living, so can you. You can become one of the highest-paid people in the world simply by focusing on becoming very good at selling. It will open every door for you.

Sales—The Seven-Part Recipe

1. Prospecting.
2. Building rapport and trust with the person you are talking to.
3. The Diagnostic Phase
4. The Presentation
5. Answering objections
6. Close the sale
7. Get resales and referrals

Chapter Eight

How to Increase the Value of Every Relationship

~

It may sound strange to use the words *productivity* and *relationships* in the same sentence, since the two concepts seem so different. When one thinks of productivity, one thinks of efficiency, maximizing the output from every input, and getting results. When one thinks of relationships, one thinks of complexity, sensitivity, emotional connections, and quality time. The two ideas seem very different.

In fact, there are some aspects of relationships where the idea of productivity does apply and can actually enhance the relationship. In other aspects, it definitely does not apply and can erode the relationship. It's critical to understand the difference between the two.

Let's begin by discussing where productivity can enhance our relationships. This is particularly true in our professional lives interacting with others in the workplace.

Going back to all the work that I've done in forty or fifty years, we find what we call *mastermind relationships*, where two or more people get together to share ideas, working toward a common goal. The common goal can just be each other's best interest.

On the first day of my coaching program I say, "The very first thing you do when you go home from this course is you form your first mastermind relationship. You find four or five people who work in different industries, you invite them to join a business mastermind, and you have them all join you for breakfast or lunch at a nearby restaurant.

"Then you say, 'One of the best ways to move ahead in our lives is to share ideas with other people who are ambitious, aggressive, and working ahead in their lives. Let's get together once a week, and we will take one question. It could be attracting more business, or it could be balancing work time with family time, or something else. We'll share ideas, and we'll do this on a weekly basis. How do you feel about that?'"

You could have a mastermind in which people just get together and shoot the breeze, or you could have a mastermind that's focused on a specific question.

A friend of mind formed a mastermind in which they took a success book, and everybody read the book that week. They had their mastermind meeting from 6:30 to 8:00 in the morning at a nearby restaurant, and they had one person who was assigned to review the book for the entire group. Then everybody asked questions about the book.

People were invited to join the mastermind on the condition that they read the book and participate in the meetings. So it was very clear. If you weren't going to read the book, or if it

---

Mastermind relationships **are where two or more people get together to share ideas, working toward a common goal.**

---

became clear in the meeting that you hadn't read the book, you would be uninvited.

People said their lives changed forever with that mastermind. Every one of them lurched ahead in their careers, their incomes went up, their satisfaction went up, and their happiness went up. It was absolutely amazing. The doctor that organized the mastermind became one of the most respected people in his community, and one of the wealthiest as well.

What's the purpose of a mastermind? Napoleon Hill found that every talented person was successful to a certain degree. After they started to get together on a regular basis with one or more talented executives, their businesses exploded. There were people like Rockefeller and Henry Ford and Thomas Edison. All of these people got together in masterminds with other people like themselves.

In my classes, people would say that, even with complete strangers who were top executives in the community, they never asked anyone to join a mastermind that didn't say yes. They all loved the idea of a mastermind.

The time that you spend together with other people who are in different fields but who also want to be successful is some of the most productive time you'll have in your life. For many people, it's been the difference between wealth and poverty, between struggling and becoming the top people in their industry.

Significant Others

Your relationships at home and with your spouse are the most important of all. What is the goal of a relationship with a significant other? That's very simple. To be happier than you were outside the relationship. It's to work together in such a way that both of you benefit far more than if you were not in the relationship at all.

You know you're in a good relationship when your significant other is your best friend. You know when you're ready to get married because you have met your best friend. There's no one else you'd want to be with or to talk to or to go on vacations with or to play golf with. It's this person.

A relationship must be valuable to each person. Each person in the relationship is committed to helping the other improve the quality of their life or work.

How do you do that? To repeat an earlier point, the major obstacle between where you are today and where you want to be is always a problem of some kind. Your job is to help people identify the problems, obstacles, and constraints that are holding them back from fulfilling their full potential.

Your job as a parent is to help your children to fulfill their potential by helping them overcome their obstacles, solve their

---

The goal of a relationship with a significant other:
1. To be happier than you were outside the relationship.
2. You work together so both of you benefit more
than if you were not in the relationship at all.
3. To be each other's best friend.

---

problems, and achieve their goals. Your job is to do exactly the right things for them.

There's nothing more important in relationships than time. The value of a relationship is in direct proportion to the amount of time that you spend face-to-face with the other person. Relationships between husbands and wives and significant others are happy in direct proportion to the amount of time you spend talking to the other.

One great time management principle is leave things off. Leave the television off, leave the computer off, leave things off when you come home from work. Just focus 100 percent on the other person. Ask the other person about what they did today, how things worked out, and what they're working on. This is extremely important. Talk to and ask questions of the other person before you wait for them to ask questions of you.

Most men—and I have been guilty of this in the past—think their day at work was the most fascinating expenditure of time since Christ walked the earth. Women have very interesting lives as well. Men should ask women about their lives: "What did you do today? Then what did you do?"

Similarly, the greatest question of all to keep a conversation in a mastermind productive and important is say, "What did you do? What did you do this morning? Then what did you do?" When the person is talked out, they can ask you questions, and you can answer.

The best way to build your children so that they're strong and positive and confident is to remember that you are the most influential person in their lives. Make sure to take a great interest in your children, and make them feel valuable and important and wonderful about themselves.

When you come home at night, go to your children and spend ten to fifteen minutes asking them about their day. Instead of talking, which is what most parents do, or dispensing knowledge as if they were wise people, just say, "How did the day go? What did you do at school? How is everything? What kind of problems are you wrestling with? Is there anything that I can do to help you?"

Another suggestion: get down on the same level. If your children are sitting down, sit down. If your children are on the floor, get down on the floor. You always want to be at eye level with the people you are talking to. In business, in masterminds, and every other situation, make sure that you are at eye level, because that's the only way two people can communicate together.

Productivity in relationships means that you want every minute that you spend with another person to be valuable for both of you. You share ideas, insights, and experiences. You share ways of solving and overcoming problems and resolving or removing constraints.

The most important thing in relationships is to think in terms of benefits. What benefits do you want to enjoy from a relationship with another person? The more you enjoy those relationships, of course, the more productive the relationship is and the more valuable it is to you.

My relationship with my wife is the most valuable time spent in my whole life. Everything else is secondary to that. Not only do I think that, I tell her that all the time, and she knows it without a question.

My kids know how important they are to me. I tell them all the time, "You are more important to me than anything else in the world." Each of my children knows that and says, "I know,

---

**Productivity in relationships means you want
every minute that you spend with another person
to be valuable for both of you.**

Dad. I know I am." There's never been a doubt about that in all the years we've been together.

Productivity in relationships means that you take the time to remove misunderstandings, doubts, and difficulties, and that you're wide open. I look upon myself as my children's mentor and as the head of the mastermind. We work together, talk together, and share our work and skills together.

My children's incomes, standard of living, marriages, and child raising are their work, so I spend a lot of time with them on these things. How can I help them? How can I guide them, direct them, and open doors for them? They can see that I am intimately involved with their quality of life.

I also spend a lot of time on my relationship with their spouses. I make them feel they are really important to me. I talk to my children about what excellent people they have in their lives, what excellent choices they've made.

One measure of a good relationship is that everybody laughs all the time. When we get together, everybody laughs together. The kids laugh, the grown children laugh, the spouses laugh. When you talk about productivity in a relationship, I say the key question is how much you laugh together.

As I said earlier, there's nothing more important for making a relationship productive and valuable than face time—face-to-face, head-to-head, knee-to-knee, heart-to-heart—when you take the time to ask questions and listen. The more you listen, the more the person likes you, trusts you, believes in you, and opens up to you.

For managers or business leaders, the best thing you can say to your workers is, "How are you doing? How's everything at home? How's everything with the kids?" These questions are so open-ended that they can answer at a deep level of intimacy, or at a shallow level.

You also can follow up. Remember this: if you ask a question and you don't follow up, it means that you were not really interested in the answer. Ask, "How's everything going?" and the other person tells you. Say, "How did that happen?" or, "What did you do when you heard that?" or, "What are you going to do now?"

Follow-up questions imprint on the other person that you're deeply interested in what they're doing.

Many managers think, "I'm so busy. I don't have time to hunker down around the campfire with my staff and have long chats." But it doesn't take very long. It's just a natural part of your work life to say, "How is everything going? Is there anything I can do to help you? What are your plans for the future?"

I'll give you an example. In my company, I've said, "We want you to be happy. Everybody here should be happy. If you're not happy for any reason, then come to the other managers or me, tell us what it is, and we'll change it if we possibly can. We don't want you to be unhappy. If we can't make you happy, or if you think you'd be happier somewhere else, then you should go there. Work with other people, or do something different."

Over the years, everybody has learned that it's OK to be ready to move on. They have done as much as they can. They've reached the top of what we can offer them. They go out, and they get another job. When they do, we take them out for lunch.

We celebrate their moving onward and upward, so nobody feels they have to sneak around and talk to people on the sly.

Our employees say, "I'm applying for this other job, and if I can get it, it'll enable me to use my existing skills at a higher level." We say, "Great." We give them referrals and testimonials, and we help them in every way possible to take the next step in their lives. It's amazing how happy people are when they know that they can be open and honest with everybody, especially the boss. That's a productive relationship.

Tips for relationships of all kinds

1. There's nothing more important in relationships than time.
2. Turn off distractions and focus 100% on the other person.
3. Tell all close family members and spouses, "you are more important to me than anything else in the world."
4. Remove misunderstandings, doubts and difficulties. Stay completely transparent.
5. Find ways to add humor to your relationships—a sign of a good relationship is laughter.
6. Ask open-ended questions, and follow-up questions to show the person you are deeply interested in them.

Conclusion

Make a Difference!

One of the most common questions is, "What kind of a difference do you want to make in your world in the course of your lifetime?" As it happens, everybody wants to make a difference. Everybody wants to be important. Everybody wants to be a person of value and to be liked and respected by other people.

Wonderfully enough, we are designed in such a way that if you do something that you really like doing, you work with people you really enjoy being with, and do your job really well, every possibility will open up for you. People will enjoy your company, they will help you to achieve your goals, and they will open doors for you, so that you become more valuable and you'll do your job even better.

It's also important for you to have personal goals and targets and to make lists. Look upon yourself as a very valuable and important person. As a valuable and important person, you must organize your life and your activities so that you produce the most possible for yourself and the most important people in your life.

Whenever you are doing something that's important to you, and you're making progress and moving towards your most important goals, you feel happy about yourself. You have more energy, your self-esteem goes up, and your self-confidence goes up. You bounce back faster. You have more resilience. You are also admired and respected by the people around you.

So this is your job—to fulfill your destiny as a human being. Only you can decide what that is. Then write it down, make a plan, and work on it all the time. Get better and better at doing the most important things that you need to do in order to be the happiest person you can possibly be.

Printed in the USA
CPSIA information can be obtained
at www.ICGtesting.com
JSHW012028140824
68134JS00033B/2925